UNEP Studies   Volume 3

The African Child
and His Environment

UNEP Studies

A previous publication within the scope of this series was published directly by UNEP, but is available from Pergamon Press:

TECHNOLOGY, DEVELOPMENT AND THE ENVIRONMENT:
A RE-APPRAISAL
A. K. N. Reddy

The African Child and His Environment

Editors

R. OGBONNA OHUCHE

BARNABAS OTAALA

for the Science Education Programme for Africa (SEPA)

with the assistance of the
UNITED NATIONS ENVIRONMENT PROGRAMME (UNEP)

Published for the
United Nations Environment Programme
by
PERGAMON PRESS

Oxford · New York · Toronto · Sydney · Paris · Frankfurt

U.K.	Pergamon Press Ltd., Headington Hill Hall, Oxford OX3 0BW, England
U.S.A.	Pergamon Press Inc., Maxwell House, Fairview Park, Elmsford, New York 10523, U.S.A.
CANADA	Pergamon of Canada, Suite 104, 150 Consumers Road, Willowdale, Ontario M2J 1P9, Canada
AUSTRALIA	Pergamon Press (Aust.) Pty. Ltd., PO Box 544, Potts Point, NSW 2011, Australia
FRANCE	Pergamon Press SARL, 24 rue des Ecoles, 75240 Paris, Cedex 05, France
FEDERAL REPUBLIC OF GERMANY	Pergamon Press GmbH, 6242 Kronberg-Taunus, Hammerweg 6, Federal Republic of Germany

First edition **1981**

British Library Cataloguing in Publication Data

The African Child and His Environment. – (United
    Nations Environment Programme. UNEP studies; vol. 3).
    1. Child psychology – Africa 2. Man – Influence
    of environment – Africa
    I. Ohuche, R Ogbonna II. Otaala, Barnabas
    III. Science Education Programme for Africa
    155.4   BF721   79–41301

    ISBN 0–08–025671–6

Set in 10 on 12 Press Roman by
Express Litho Service (Oxford)
Printed and bound in Great Britain by
William Clowes (Beccles) Limited, Beccles and London

PREFACE

THIS book is the product of a contract between the United Nations Environmental Programme (UNEP) and the Science Education Programme for Africa (SEPA) which was signed in April 1978. Through this contract UNEP enabled SEPA to retain the services of consultants to survey thirteen African countries to find out what services are available to children and assess previous investigations regarding them in these countries. The study was commissioned to present a true picture of the child's environment in sub-Saharan Africa. The three consultants were then joined by three specialists at a one-week meeting to draft a report to be published by UNEP as a major contribution to the activities of the International Year of the Child (IYC).

Selected for the survey were Professor Barnabas Otaala, then Head of the Department of Educational Psychology, Kenyatta University College, for East and Southern Africa; Dr Pierre Dasen, then of the Bureau of Educational Research, University of Nairobi, for Francophone Africa; and Dr R. Ogbonna Ohuche, Department of Education, University of Nigeria, for Anglophone West Africa. The three other specialists selected were Dr Hubert M. Dyasi, then Programme Director, SEPA; Dr Elizabeth Etuk Eke, Department of Education, University of Nigeria; and Dr Isa Omari, Head of the Department of Education, University of Dar es Salaam.

Thirteen countries were surveyed. Botswana, Kenya, Mauritius, and Zambia were surveyed by Professor Otaala and the United Republic of Tanzania by Dr Daniel Kiminyo, on behalf of Professor Otaala. Ghana, Liberia, Nigeria, and Sierra Leone were surveyed by Dr Ohuche. The Ivory Coast, Senegal, Upper Volta, and Zaire were surveyed by Dr Dasen.

They wrote individual reports which were pieced together in Nairobi during a two-week meeting in November, 1978. The meeting was attended by the seven aforementioned specialists (including Dr Kiminyo), plus Dr Marian Addy, Acting Programme Director, SEPA. The second week of the

v

meeting was possible because of a one-week workshop organized by SEPA, following the meeting of the specialists. The topic of the workshop was conceptual functioning among African children.

As Chairperson of the team, I would like to acknowledge the contributions made by all the participants especially those of Drs Eke, and Dasen. At certain stages during the development of the manuscript it became necessary to seek the services of other specialists. In this regard, I would like to acknowledge the contributions made by Mrs Kalu of the Department of Education, and Mrs Nwana of the Department of Health and Physical Education, University of Nigeria. Mrs Kalu's unpublished article on the Social Environment of the West African Child, and Mrs Nwana's unpublished articles on the Physical and Health Environment of the African Child, both drafted at my request, were used freely by the editors.

I would like to add that towards the end of the first week of our meeting in Nairobi we had a most enlightening discussion with Drs V. O. I. Johnson and P. Mwanza of UNEP. It is my pleasure to thank them on behalf of the team for their contributions to the manuscript. Thanks are also due to the participants of the Workshop on Conceptual Functioning Among African Children for the ideas they contributed. The participants were: Drs Marian Addy, George Collinson, Pierre Dasen, Elizabeth Etu Eke, Allieu Kamara, Daniel Kiminyo, R. Ogbonna Ohuche, Barnabas Otaala, Robert Pearson, E. Molapi Sebatane, Mrs Leah Ngini and Mr Hamid Sinuff.

The consultants acknowledge with immense gratitude the cooperation of officials of ministries and government functionaries in the thirteen countries visited. The Kenya Institute of Education (K. I. E.) is to be thanked for being a good host to the planning meeting. Gratitude is also due to the numerous typists at the Kenya Institute of Education, Kenyatta University College, UNEP and the University of Nigeria, Nsukka who typed the various drafts.

Finally, the two contracting organizations UNEP and SEPA deserve Africa's and our deep appreciation for their foresight which has singled out Africa for special consideration. Humble as this effort is, we, the contributors, have reason to believe that it will lead Africa to useful future endeavours and greater heights.

Nairobi   R. OGBONNA OHUCHE
                                                  Department of Education
                                                  University of Nigeria
                                                  Nsukka, Nigeria.

CONTENTS

This is Furahisha from Wayingombe, a semi-arid area in Tanzania, carrying water from a local river to make bricks for building a village community school together with her schoolmates.
Credit: A. Vollan, UNICEF

Ali from Somalia playing with his friends in the streets of Mogadishu, Somalia. Credit: E. Thorning, UNICEF

Nalemba from Kenya proudly carrying her little contented brother when she goes out to play with her friends. Credit: E. Thorning, UNICEF

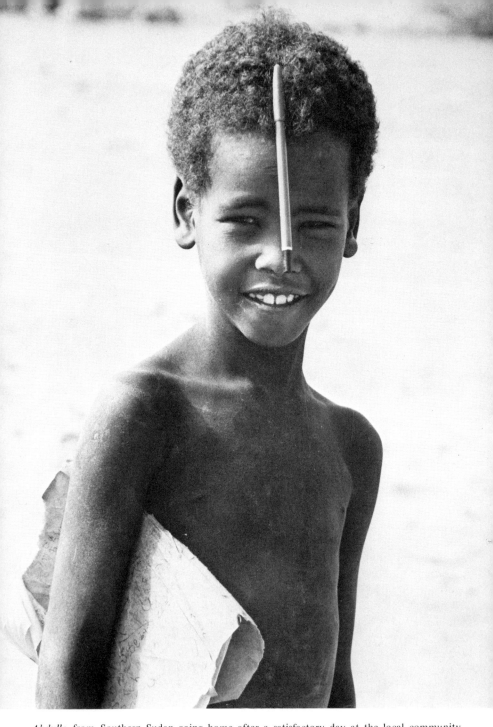

Abdulla from Southern Sudan going home after a satisfactory day at the local community school. Credit: W. Cambell, UNICEF

1

INTRODUCTION

IN THE forthcoming chapters we shall describe the child in an African environment. It is necessary to begin with some comments about heredity, the nature of the environment, and the interaction between heredity and environment.

HEREDITY

It is obvious that individuals differ from one another. The source of this difference is not only the genetic structure of an individual, but also the environment in which the individual has developed. We will clarify what is meant by heredity, and the nature of the environment.

The heredity of an individual fundamentally consists of two sets of genes received from his parents at the time of conception. When we say that a certain influence or trait is "hereditary" we mean that such an influence or trait can ultimately be traced to a particular gene inherited from the parents.

At the time of conception many gene combinations are possible; this almost unlimited variety of possible gene combinations is the basis of individual difference. From this observation we note that no two children from the same parents, not even fraternal twins, have identical heredity. It is only in the case of identical twins, who develop from the division of a single fertilized ovum, that we find identical sets of genes. Those individuals (identical twins) are exact replicas with regard to heredity.

THE NATURE OF ENVIRONMENT

We must differentiate between the popular definition and the psychological definition of environment. Environment, popularly defined, is usually confined to a geographical attribute. This definition is inadequate, for it cannot be concluded that two siblings, brought up under the same roof, have the same psychological environment, even though they inhabit the same geographical environment.

Psychologically, environment "consists of the sum total of the stimulation the individual receives from conception until death." (Anastasi, 1958, p. 64.) This is an active concept of environment. It implies that the physical presence of objects does not constitute environment, unless the objects serve as stimuli for the individual.

This definition takes into account all aspects which constitute environment, and covers a life span from conception until death. For it has repeatedly been shown that the individual's development is determined by the environment which influences him *in utero*. The diet of the mother, the supply, or lack of proper nutrition, certain hormonal secretions from the glands, drugs, and other conditions do have a profound and lasting effect on the development of the child.

INTERACTION OF HEREDITY AND ENVIRONMENT

We shall now examine the relationship that exists between heredity and the environment. It is now commonly believed that every trait that an individual has, and every reaction that he demonstrates, can in the final analysis, be attributed to his heredity and to his environment.

Disregarding the characteristics inherited at birth, the development of a child, which includes the physical expression of the genetic materials that make up the child, is very much influenced by the environment in which he lives. The influence is not simple, but a complex interaction in which the type of character inherited greatly determines its propensity towards change by environmental influences.

The most widely and currently accepted view of the relationship between heredity and environment is that of interaction. This does not mean that the effects of heredity and environment are cumulative or additive. Rather, it means that the nature and extent of the influence of each factor (hereditary or environmental) depends upon the contribution of the other. "In other words, any one environmental factor will exert a different influence depending upon the specific hereditary material upon which it operates. Similarly, any hereditary factor will operate differently under different environmental conditions." (Anastasi, 1958, pp. 68–9) This concept of interaction fits in meaningfully with Piaget's theory of development in children. (Flavell, 1963.) There are other theories put forward by other psychologists, but it is beyond the scope of this work to provide an exhaustive coverage of the field. We have chosen to refer to Piaget's theory because there is a growing body of information in Africa, accumulated from Piagetian research.

In the interactionist theory, Piaget sees life as a continuous creative interaction between the person and his environment. His key concept is adaptation. This interaction between the person and the environment functions outwardly as adaptive coping, and inwardly as organization.

Piaget perceives the adaptive interaction between the organism and the environment to involve two complementary processes: assimilation and accommodation.

Assimilation involves the inner organization of the individual; the organism utilizes something from the environment and incorporates it into the internal organism. For example, the eating of food, which when digested becomes part of the organism. Similarly, as experience in the environment is mentally digested by the child, it becomes part of his inner self. The child sees unfamiliar things in the context of the familiar. Whenever the child encounters a new situation, he reacts to those elements of it that are familiar with the same behaviour patterns he has used for similar situations in the past.

Accommodation, the complementary process to assimilation, involves the ability of the organism to adjust to the specific contours of the object it is trying to assimilate. To extend the food metaphor, accommodation involves opening of the mouth, chewing, swallowing and digestion. Variations in environmental circumstances challenge the child; and as the child copes with them, he changes his repertoire of existing tools to accommodate new modes of behaviour.

The concept of adaptation, including the processes of assimilation and accommodation, provided the theoretical foundation for Piaget's research, in which he carried out innumerable tests and experiments with children of different age groups.

We shall attempt to elaborate on the subject of the African child and his environment and to explain how he is affected by the nature of his changing environment. We shall also discuss the concern that exists in African countries, in governments and among organizations for the benefit of the African child.

AFRICAN EDUCATIONAL PROBLEMS

African countries, like many developing nations spend an average of approximately thirty per cent of recurrent expenditure on education and other services related to the welfare of the child. In spite of the large and rapidly growing investments in education, we witness increasing disparity between the needs of the children and the resources available to them. At the end of the 1960s, the percentage of GNP invested in education by developing countries was comparable to that of the USA, Europe, and the USSR; and in terms of percentage of public budget, it was even higher.

Between 1960 and 1970, the developing countries increased their public expenditure for education by approximately a hundred and seventeen per cent. During the same period, their school enrolments increased by about a hundred per cent. (Because of the population explosion, however, the percentage of children enrolled, out of all the school-age children increased by less than ten per cent.) By the end of this decade, approximately half the population of these countries will have attended school, less than thirty per cent will have gone to secondary school, and less than three per cent will have received higher education. Thus, despite major efforts and huge investments in education, the gap between educational needs and resources continues to widen.

The dilemma arises from several factors, including the following: growing populations and increasing popular demand for services concurrent with inadequate funds for development; inadequate knowledge about practical alternatives in fundings, efficiency, and measurement of outputs in education; and archaic and rigid methods of education where the scholastic content does not meet the changing demands of social, economic, or political developments; and where it does not take into account the intellectual development of the child or the cultural environment in which he lives.

As a result of the realization of the inadequacy of the current system of education, many African countries have organized Curriculum Development

Centres to create curricula more relevant to the immediate environment of the school. In addition, during the last decade, many African countries have made great efforts to develop mathematics, science and social studies curricula more relevant to the immediate environment of the school. Furthermore, during the last decade, many African countries have made great efforts to develop mathematics, science and social studies curricula for primary schools that are modern in approach and better adapted to the local environment than those previously imported from outside of Africa.

At a number of educational conferences the importance of collaborative efforts among educators, psychologists, curriculum workers and other groups has been emphasized. In 1967, Professor L. J. Lewis and his collaborators presented a paper to the United Nations Advisory Committee on the Application of Science and Technology to Development, in which they drew attention to the need for links to be established and maintained between those engaged in work in educational and developmental psychology and those engaged in teacher education and curriculum development. In the following year a survey of work done in the field concerning the attainment and abilities of African children was presented by Professor K. Lovell at the Sixth Leverhulme Inter-University Conference in Africa, held in Malawi. One year later, the importance of linking studies to the learning process and curriculum development in science was again noted, at the planning meeting for UNESCO's Integrated Science Teaching Programme in 1969.

In September 1974, UNESCO and UNICEF organized a workshop on the development of science and mathematics concepts in children in Africa. The workshop brought together African scholars in educational and developmental psychology, and those concerned with curriculum development. The objectives of the workshop were:

   (a) to share knowledge of the work that has been carried out, in the field of concept development in science and mathematics in children, particularly in African countries;

   (b) to plan the development of studies in concept formation in the context of the specific environment and conditions existing within African countries;

   (c) to consider the manner in which results of the studies in the learning process may be utilized in practical curriculum developmental work; and

   (d) to make suggestions for future activities, including:

—specific research programmes in the learning process,

—more effective linking of research findings and curriculum development work,

—the implications for teacher education of research findings in learning process.

In April 1978, UNEP's Programme Activity Centre for Environmental Education and Training (PACEET) commissioned the Science Education Programme for Africa (SEPA), to collect, compile, and publish studies concerning the African child and what has affected him in his environment. The publication was to: "review the present situation regarding child development, interactions in the physical, social and cultural milieu, . . . on the basis of the state-of-the-art, evaluate the quality of the delivery systems of children's benefits, and outline plans and programmes which UNEP (through PACEET) should support in pursuance of the long-term objective of promoting environmentally sound programmes beneficial to children." (p. 3, project agreement between PACEET and SEPA.) The following chapters present the results of this study, as collected and compiled by SEPA.

THE BOOK IN OUTLINE

In reading through the chapters the reader should bear in mind that Anglophone and Francophone Africa is vast: geographically, climatically, and culturally. This being the case, whatever is stated about any particular country may not be generally true about a group of countries and may not be true in another specific country.

In Chapter 2, the physical and health environment in which the child grows from conception is described. What emerges is that in African environments there are many conditions and diseases, including communicable diseases, and diseases due to dietary deficiencies, which hinder the optimal development of the child. Despite this, society had developed ways of coping best with this environment.

Various countries are in different stages of grappling with the problem of the improvement of the physical and health environment. Some are at advanced stages in the solution of the problem, and others are just realizing the importance of a good physical and health environment in the healthy growth and development of the child.

Chapter 3 deals with the social environment. In it we find that there were traditions in Africa supportive of the old social structure. Social changes, including technological, economic, and structural changes, and ideological values from outside have had considerable impact on the old structure. Despite these changes, when one examines African societies today, one notices the persistence and continuity of the prominent values and practices of the old order.

Chapter 4 gives an indication of educational services provided by various African countries. Information is provided on the extent and operational policies of, pre-school and day care services, and on primary, and secondary education. The picture that emerges is one of phenomenal increase in numbers of children going to school. What also emerges is that, despite these increases, because of rapid population growth in many African countries, especially in the age group of 0–15 years, even larger numbers of African youth never see the walls of a classroom.

In addition to the educational services described in the previous chapter, Chapter 5 describes other services provided by various government and private organizations, for the welfare of children and youth. These include recreational services and activities designed to enable youths to acquire skills that will provide them with gainful employment after training.

Chapter 6 describes the characteristics of child development and the environmental factors affecting it. The developments which take place during the neonatal and postnatal stages, including physical, psychomotor, and emotional development, are surveyed in several African countries.

Chapter 7 indicates the many interesting studies carried out in Africa on intellectual development. It points out that the "basic intellectual mechanisms are universal, but the environment determines the situations in which they are applicable". The rest of the chapter deals specifically with Piagetian studies that have been conducted in Africa in this special area.

Finally, in Chapter 8, in the light of the state-of-the-art provided in the previous chapters, we deal with prospects, observations, and recommendations. Our hope is that governments, and other agencies, will find this chapter particularly useful as a source of information for possible future action, in developing programmes for the welfare of the child.

2

THE PHYSICAL AND HEALTH ENVIRONMENTS

INTRODUCTION

In this chapter, an attempt is made to describe the physical and health environments within which the child in Africa grows, and in which he undergoes informal, and sometimes formal, education. The environment is viewed within the context of the immediate surroundings of the child, which include his home, the neighbourhood in which he lives, his village or town, and their physical and social dimensions.

Our approach is to consider that the child's immediate environment starts soon after conception, and to highlight some crucial stages beginning with the intrauterine period, going through infancy, early childhood, into adolescence. We should emphasize that some of the statements about the physical conditions, the climate, and social practices are general to most parts of Africa; others, however, may be true of only some specific parts, or countries, in Africa.

THE INTRAUTERINE ENVIRONMENT

The health of any child begins to be determined during pregnancy, from the intrauterine stage of life, where the foundation of health is laid. It is therefore pertinent, in considering the environment of the child, to trace his physical environment from the womb. This approach is especially applicable in the case of the African child, because of the poor nutritional state of many African mothers.

The diet of a mother during her own childhood, and during pregnancy, influences the child's development. In many instances, the nutritional state of pregnant women in Africa is below optimum. The chances of the foetus for adequate development in such a case follow. The poor nutritional state of the mother provides a weak foundation for the establishment of a sound physique, and initial and long-term health. A poorly nourished mother is more likely to go into premature labour or to produce an immature baby, than a mother who is properly nourished.

In addition, many drugs pass readily through the placenta of the foetus, some of which are potentially dangerous to the health or physical development of the baby. Sedative drugs, such as morphine, are known to cause the baby to be lethargic at birth. The tragedy caused by thalidomide is well known throughout the world. The effects on the foetus and the mother, of some of the medicinal herbs consumed by African women, during pregnancy and labour, are not yet known, but it is not difficult to imagine that some of them may be harmful.

THE DELIVERY ENVIRONMENT

While in the womb, the child enjoys a relatively sheltered life, despite the potential dangers already mentioned. Delivery will take place in one of three broadly defined environments: by the traditional birth attendant, at the maternity home, or in the maternity ward of a hospital.

In general, before the attainment of independence by most African countries, the common manner of delivery was by the traditional birth attendant, either at her home, or at the home of the pregnant woman. Recent practice has begun to favour the use of the other two alternatives. Yet many problems still exist which force pregnant women to resort to traditional birth attendants. These include poor economic circumstances, the unavailability of proper facilities in rural areas, and underdeveloped transportation and other communication services.

In some parts of Nigeria, for example, when labour is about to commence, the pregnant woman, accompanied by an older female relative, usually her mother, treks to the home of the traditional birth attendant. There, she takes her place on a mat, or a wooden bed with a mat as bedsheet, and is given a cupful of the attendant's labour mixture to drink. The drink is expected to help her reach the advanced stage of labour by aiding the contractions of the uterine muscles. Delivery by this method is safe, providing no complications arise. When the foetus is expelled, the placenta is cut. Educating the traditional birth attendants as to the necessity of proper sanitary conditions will improve this system of delivery, which, with all of the variety in its execution, is the only system available to many of the women in rural Africa. The Danfa Rural Project in Ghana aims at just this type of education.

Again using Nigeria as an example, we find that a maternity home normally has a midwife who is trained in the technique of delivering babies. When the woman arrives with her relative, at the initial stages of labour the midwife asks for a razor blade, which will later be used to cut the umbilical cord. At the delivery there is a trolley, which has two pairs of artery forceps, a kidney dish, and a bowl with wool swabs in it. If there are no complications, delivery is accomplished without major problems.

It is now the case in most sub-Saharan African countries that all towns and some rural areas have hospitals. Facilities available in each hospital are linked with the state of economic and social development of both the nation and the particular area of that nation in which the hospital is established. The average hospital would have both antenatal services and a maternity ward for purposes of delivery and immediate postnatal care. Pregnant women are encouraged to use available antenatal services, and hospitals are discouraging to those who fail to do so and only report to the hospital at the onset of labour.

On the whole, both human and material resources in maternity wards can at times be hard pressed. At some times, especially at night, when the rate of delivery tends to be high, there may be only one ward midwife overseeing the attention given to all of the women in labour, who could be as many as ten in some hospitals. The gynaecologist is called in only for cases which appear to have complications beyond those the ward sister considers herself capable of handling. But even the hospitals are sometimes ill-equipped to handle emergency situations. For example, it is usual that blood banks are not properly developed. In cases where blood is needed, relations of the woman in labour must try to find someone who will either donate or sell the required type of blood.

THE HEALTH ENVIRONMENT OF THE INFANT AND PRE-SCHOOL CHILD

It is possible that the African child will grow up in a town but more probable that he will grow up in a rural area. In rural areas, members of the same clan or kindred live close to one another in villages, and share amenities such as the stream, the market, and the school. The villages are organized with regard to the cleaning of streams, the sweeping of the market square, and the maintenance of roads and other amenities which are available to the entire community. For example, each family unit is responsible for the disposal of its own refuse, which is usually utilized as manure for farm crops.

It is one of the ironies of modern African life that the rural areas where the majority of the children in Africa are born and raised tend to be neglected by the governments. Medical services, for the most part, are limited to those that can be provided with little or no training in the dispensing and administration of drugs. Basic infrastructural facilities do not exist. Communication systems are underdeveloped, and employment opportunities generally, do not exist.

One result of this neglect of the villages is the migration of the population toward the few available urban centres, most of which are overcrowded. The African urban centre is a complicated phenomenon. A working definition is that a town is any large community which is not a village. It is generally true that in each country, whatever facilities exist are concentrated in the towns, but the amenities within the towns vary with the importance of the town, and within the sections in each town.

For the children who live in the better-developed sections of the town, living conditions are sanitary and health promoting. In many African towns, however, the greater number of children live in the peri-urban and slum sections of the town. Here living conditions are harsh, with running water hardly available. When taps are available, in or near the building in which they live, water may run only occasionally.

In some African countries, an omnibus refuse bin is usually situated at one end of the street. The bin may be properly constructed with prescribed dimensions, or it may be improvised. The bin is supposed to be emptied periodically by the Local Council, but sometimes remains unemptied for days resulting in an overflow of refuse.

This type of environment is hardly conducive to the development of optimum physical and emotional health. It is likely to be associated with a high incidence of communicable diseases. The commonest causes of morbidity and mortality in infants and pre-school children include diarrhoea, dysentery, fevers, and a diverse selection of diseases caused by bacteria and other organisms which thrive in such an environment. These conditions and others, which generally affect children, are readily discouraged by hygienic and preventive measures, such as immunization (although immunization agents are hardly ever available at the time they are required).

THE PHYSICAL ENVIRONMENT OF THE SCHOOL CHILD

It has been noted that the physical environment of the pre-school child is dominated by his home. Gradually, but surely, this environment expands until at the age of six years, when he is expected to start school, it includes his home, his village or town, their physical and social dimensions and inter-relationships. In this context, the neighbourhood where he plays with his peers, the market, whether it be the village, town, or roadside market, the school and the church or mosque stand out.

The market is a peculiar phenomenon in Africa. Early in his life, the child in Africa gets involved in buying and selling. Even the children of the elite occasionally have to pack up sweets and sundries from the roadside market. Children who do not attend school must walk long distances to sell farm products or other goods. Many of those who do attend school also must help their parents or close relatives in the market or shop when the school day is over. They may have difficulty with adding or subtracting numbers in school, but usually do not make mistakes with change in the market place or shop.

Another feature that stands out in the village is the village school. It is generally simply constructed − one or two long buildings, which may not be permanently partitioned into rooms. There are usually some benches and blackboards. Books are difficult to obtain and audiovisual aids are rare. The headmaster or headmistress may not have an office and the school is fortunate if there is a store where the valuable school materials can be locked up. Otherwise they must be carried by school children to the headmaster's house at the end of each school day. Still, the school occupies a prominent place in the life of the village.

In contrast to the village school, are the schools in town. Two basic types of in-town schools are distinguishable. One is the prestigious school with relatively well trained teachers and good facilities, where class sizes are small. The other type is public, and usually located in the high density area of town.

Invariably, its facilities are overextended and its classes are overcrowded. The range of abilities in any class is wide as would be expected. Even so, these overcrowded public schools generally have better trained, more experienced teachers than the village schools do.

Regardless of distinction, the schools of Africa have inherited some common unenviable characteristics. They have lost the finest qualities of traditional African education, which was functional in operation and environmentally based. Instead, the modern school has become a place where abstract theoretical work, not necessarily associated with reality, is dealt with. The concept of using school education to stimulate children to ask questions about the world around them is discussed in our faculties and colleges of education, but it is merely discussion. The schools are mainly utilized as places where children memorize static information provided by teachers, some of whom are just able to keep abreast of their pupils. Attitudes and habits are hardly expected to be affected by schooling.

In some countries, the majority of the secondary schools are boarding rather than neighbourhood schools. The environmental conditions in the dormitories are usually different from those in the homes of the pupils. Dormitory conditions may change, or contribute to changes in the attitude among boarding school students.

CONCLUSION

This chapter has attempted to present the reader with an insight into the physical and health environment of the child in Africa. Beginning with the intrauterine environment, the chapter introduces and comments on the delivery environment, the pre-school environment, and the school environment. The complication due to the vastness and heterogeneity of the African continent, demands that we only highlight some common features, and run the risk of over-simplification or exaggeration. We shall now continue to discuss the social environment of the child in Africa.

3

THE SOCIAL ENVIRONMENT

IT IS evident that when technological, economic, social structural and ideological conditions change, the values, beliefs, and life styles of the affected generation also change and that these changes have a profound impact on the way new generations are socialized. Africa has witnessed rapid socioeconomic change, which is partially explained by the new politics ushered in by independence. The world-view held by traditional societies, which supported the old social structure, has come under attack as education, radio, and Western consumer cultures have invaded villages. The intriguing aspect of Africa, however, is the persistence and continuity of tangible values and practices of the old order.

We shall now briefly examine the religious factor and the occupational factor, and how each of these affect the child. We shall also refer to the influences of the family, on the development of the social environment of the child. In each of these cases, as previously indicated, there are so many differences within the vast continent of Africa, that we can only generalize.

RELIGIOUS FACTOR

In the traditional world-view, time moves cyclically and the life of man moves along the endless cycle from birth to death to reincarnation. Death is not considered an end to existence. On the contrary, responsible dead men are endowed with more powers and become protective ancestors who cheer up the kin-group in the human world. Moreover, the world is a world alive with spirits; it is a precarious world, besieged by evil spirits. The spirit world is the home of ancestral spirits. In this perception of the world, the gods determine the course of events and the fate of men. Ritual leaders ranging from the head of the family, through the ruling chief, to the professionals, devise and perform rites and taboos to protect men from the machination of the evil spirits.

Obviously, this is a predominantly religious world-view, and this religiosity imparts a sanctity to social positions and roles. It is by the ordering of the spirits, within this world-view, that prediction and control of space-time events can best be understood. Without computers or the brains-trust approach to problems, communities resort to diviners who act as intermediaries between men and the gods. The decision-making process is influenced by the voices of oracles and diviners.

Among the new ideas, are the Islamic and Christian views of the nature of life, death, and the universe. In the old religion, the Supreme Being worked with and through innumerable minor divinities and spirits. Both Islam and Christianity are not only monotheistic, but extremely concerned with extinguishing any notion of intermediary gods. The intricate system of rituals by which the old order maintained coherence, is under attack. Rites of passage of the old order are considered pagan. Baptism, Confirmation, recitation of Catechism have replaced these. The newly introduced religions attacked the traditional culture and world-view more radically than the colonial governments. Their success is limited, as the children still operate in a tensely transitional state.

Interdenominational criticisms and rivalry, and the failure of the evangelical movement, are weakening the strong religious influences which had accompanied education. A gradual comparison of past and present beliefs, limited attempts to indigenize churches, and a search for cultural roots have resulted in an attack on the established churches, the ramifications of which have not yet been fully grasped. It seems clear that the religious cloak, whether it is Moslem or Christian, hangs lightly on many shoulders. This is especially true of the educated and the leaders to whom the young look up for guidance. The religious world-view no longer exists; it does not permeate life. nor is it easy to say whether any coherent world-view exists. Events are tackled on an *ad hoc* basis. If the new religious beliefs interfere with the cult of materialism, with the fulfilment of traditional expectations, or with the consultation of oracles concerning inexplicable disasters and illnesses, then the new beliefs must be held in abeyance.

It is within this scenario, that mobile and greatly expressive prayer houses which emphasize familiar intercessional approaches, faith healings, public confessions and purging, and guidance for specific problems through spiritual messages, are becoming more and more popular with the youth, even if they are less prestigious than the established religions. The existence of disagreement about whether to excise religious instruction from formal educational experiences completes the picture of the uncertain religious factor in the environment of the children.

OCCUPATIONAL FACTOR

Traditionally, most Africans had an occupation with which they could be identified. An important aspect of socialization was to train the child into one of the existing occupations of the area. Usually, children would follow the families' occupation as a matter of course. Traditional societies were, and still are, predominantly agricultural, but colonization, and the European quest for markets and raw materials opened Africa not only to modern technological influences and processes, but to a greater variety and level of specialization in occupations.

In many areas, the agricultural methods are unsophisticated and the farmers barely subsist by using a method of shifting cultivation. The yields are barely adequate for the needs of the family, with a little surplus to trade for non-agricultural items. Men engage in the farming of the more durable root crops and in tending animals, and women in perishable items such as vegetables. The hoe and the matchet remain the basic agricultural implements used by the small farmers, and farming tends to rely upon the rainy season, when nature provides irrigation. When there is little work to be done on the farms, the men hunt. Government, cooperative, and individual large scale farms and plantations have intervened to boost agriculture; but in many countries, food is produced in insufficient quantities and must be imported. Farming is not popular with educated children, and the migration of youth towards the urban areas, in search of other jobs, is causing concern in many countries. The establishment of schemes and farm slogans, such as the farm settlements, land armies and "operation feed the nation" underscores the desire of the administration to grow more food, and indicates disruption of the old social environment.

Other traditional occupations such as fishing, hunting, carving, weaving and pottery-making have similarly become less desirable occupations. Trade on every imaginable scale is flourishing. Education and farming appear to be incompatible. It is not convenient for the children of farmers to undertake farm work after school and during the holidays. These children constituted the labour force for the family farm. Other occupations do not suffer the same problems because children of those engaged in other occupations are able to assist after school. So, the children of farmers have either to absent themselves from school temporarily in order to farm, to avoid attending school altogether, or to attend school, often against family wishes and with a firm resolve to escape completely from the land. The skills of the other occupations are passed on to the children. Unfortunately, these occupations remain at the level of supplementary out-of-school activities, to provide additional income with which to pay fees or purchase essential commodities.

THE FAMILY

The family is one of the many facets of life influenced by the occupation of its members. Traditionally, families tended to be large to provide labour not only for the major occupation of the family, but also for the other chores that had to be attended to. What is more, the size of a man's family and the number of animals he had determined his status. In many places polygamy was common practice. At present, the situation is not very different, except among the educated group who tend to limit the size of their families. Their reasons are economic, and sometimes religious for those who contracted Christian marriages. The traditional practice of marrying more than one wife, combined with the international trend towards looser marital ties, have made the successful monogamous marriage somewhat rare. In addition, the "nouveaux riches" show off their wealth, in flamboyant cars, houses, and living styles and by increasing the size of their families.

In the rural areas, families tended to live together and provide anchorage for the young ones in all aspects of their training: in this environment the extended-family system was very strong. The role of the nuclear family was important, but the tendency was toward communalization. Any member of the extended family was a "brother" or a "sister", even if the relationship was of the seventh order. In some cases, the family ties were strengthened by intermarriage as long as very close relations, first cousins, brothers and sisters, were excluded. The situation is very much the same today. However, the extended-family ties are weakening because of economic stringencies. Families have to move in order to work in urban areas and other distant places. It is becoming increasingly difficult to "be thy brother's keeper", financially. The family can no longer maintain the habitat structure or the economic unity of the old order. Some members of the modern family leave for school when others go to the farms, and still others are away in towns doing a variety of jobs. Occasional family reunions, scheduled around Christmas or the traditional festive holidays, provide brief opportunities to hold family festivals and reinforce integrative links.

Traditional male and female roles were clearly defined in the family. The father was head of the family, responsible for certain aspects of feeding, and accommodation. His word was law. The wife was subservient to him. Her primary role was to produce and take care of children. She was expected to take care of the home while the man went out to work. The situation has changed. The increased education of women has led to greater responsibilities within the family, and corresponding demands for greater freedom.

With the disintegration of family ties, caring for the young children becomes a problem. Those in the pre-school years now must be looked after by house maids, who may or may not be relations. Older children go to school and if there is no substitute help, they stay at school, while mother goes to the farm, the market or to work. The educated working wives usually make a more durable arrangement with their hired help. The magnitude of the problem varies from country to country and with the spread of education.

PEER GROUPS, SECRET SOCIETIES, AND DANCE GROUPS

Each child in the course of his traditional development and maturity belonged to secret societies, dance groups, age grades and other informal groups. Sometimes the groups were used for work in the family farms, or for special events in the community.

The membership requirements for secret societies would vary. Some could only be joined by adults, but in many West African communities, there were and still are secret societies to which a child could belong either actively or as an honorary member. The most effective organizations for socialization are those in which the child could participate actively. An example is the *Obon* Society in the Cross-River basin of Nigeria. It holds a few secrets related to the production of the key sound in the club's exclusive dance tune. These secrets are hedged with esoteric signs which only initiates could make with their fingers. The club's dance performances are mostly at night. Females are excluded; sex differentiation is reinforced by membership. Societies also assisted in the inculcation of discipline by encouraging the maintenance of the secrets, by exposure and punishment of wrongdoing, and by providing instruction in valued skills in the guise of required tasks and dance steps. For example, endurance is cultivated by the acclamation of the one who can stay the longest period on the dance floor. This society engaged in long campaigns for human skill therefore, the process of socialization prepared the child to develop his survival instincts and to learn to endure discomfort.

In the rural areas, the younger peer groups are still organized on a familiar basis, or take the form of neighbourhood groups. These still meet on moonlit nights to practise dances and masquerades which are formally presented during festivals. Adults would visit the moonlight group practices and coach the children in the dance steps, as well as tell folk tales which embodied moral instruction and tales about the history of their locality. Boys had the additional advantage of accompanying their fathers to adult group meetings and farms where they learned the customs and bounds of their kinship through participation. Also, their fathers would call upon them to serve visitors to the house and they would invariably crouch in the corner and listen to the conversation, although good manners forbade their participation.

The older children are encouraged to form dance groups in the secondary schools for competitions at local or national levels. Those who have the aptitude and grace are allowed to participate. An important factor in African dances is that they were used as an effective method of socialization. The dances helped to develop the skills needed to function in society and were related to occupations. Thus, the riverine areas have dance steps differing from those of the hunting population, as well as from those of the agricultural or warrior groups. What is more, the groups were used to enforce discipline and inspire attributes desirable within the communities.

The age grade system which operates in some West African countries is more formal and structured than any other peer groups. This is based on three five-year age bands. Each set (and its segments) forms a distinct unit in the village; it brings together members of different *agnatic* groupings in the village. Age ranking is of considerable significance, as can be seen most clearly in the deferential behaviour of members of younger sets towards those of older ones. It breeds a sense of solidarity within the group and a healthy rivalry with other age sets, and thus mobilizes the whole village for development. A child, therefore, is brought up to perform within the genealogical kin group as well as within the general community.

Age grades were used as training ground for leadership roles and, when members became old enough, as part of the instruments of government. In recent times, however, the age grades are stronger in the traditional rural communities, although their tasks have been altered. The younger sets undertake minor cleaning jobs and the older sets build schools, hospitals, post offices, and other modern infrastructures in the communities.

LANGUAGE FACTORS

Education, and the movement toward larger economic and political organization have necessitated the use of two or more languages in African countries. Whereas previously there was no need to learn more than one language, the language of the kin-group, now African children must learn the local language or the official language of the country, in addition to their mother tongue. Many varieties of the languages are learned. In the urban areas, the "broken" version of English or French is rapidly acquired at the pre-school level, and much unlearning must be done in school. Children who learn a second language in school acquire a sense of importance in the rural setting, where they are called upon to read, write, and translate letters and other materials. The linguistic and other educational capabilities may make discipline difficult in the family, because the children may feel that their illiterate parents cannot dictate to them.

CULTURE REVIVAL

There is no doubt that many changes that have occurred have taken Africans by surprise. The traditional agencies of socialization, the family, the kin-group, social clubs and age grades are still crucial, but with modified and lessening roles. The cohesiveness of the village community is weakened by the individualism, educational and economic competition in the new order. The new religion also becomes a liability, dividing the community into quarrelsome factions. The traditional manner of earning a living is no longer adequate in the face of industry and the new technology. Traditional values of obedience, loyalty to the group, respect for elders, the dignity of manual skill, to name a few, are under attack. Even the language of the land is relegated to the background.

Formal education imparts a different world-view, characterized by a linear and chronometric perception of time which stretches out the cyclical order into a multifaceted complexity of world events. We cannot delve into the immense implications of this new world-view. It must suffice to say that it destroys the rationale behind the structure of the old order, the basic social environment. For instance, if the sperm and ova, and not the spirits, cause child conception, all the attendant ceremonies predicated on the old belief become irrelevant. Diviners and their associates are displaced. Chiefs and political leaders are still important, but the basis of their authority is no longer clothed in a spiritual aura. They are now viewed as agents of an administrative structure.

The new order is comprised of new economic, political, and religious structures and ideas. Is it possible for the old order to survive? Can there be a harmonious integration between the old and the new? The buffeting and confusion has come from lack of planning. Africans are realizing too late that certain values and institutions of the older order had merit and should not be allowed to disappear. They have also realized that change is inevitable and welcome; education and technological progress are very beneficial. The crucial question is which traditions to revive and which to discard. Judging from the famous 1977 FESTAC, more than cultural dances and attires must be retained. Serious surveys should be taken, and continental policies developed on language, values and traditional institutions. The message of FESTAC was broadcast as an appeal to come to grips with the mechanism of change, and to create a better future for the African child.

4

EDUCATIONAL SERVICES

TRADITIONAL African education was practical, informal, and primarily non-verbal. However, there existed opportunities for formal education in the secret societies, and verbal education in the folklore. In the fifteenth century, European culture began to make inroads into African culture; by the eighteenth century, Europeans and others were arriving in Africa in full force. They came as explorers, traders or missionaries. The missionary brought with him a new type of education, whose main objective was to produce persons who could study the Bible and behave as Christians. The new type of education was formal and systematic. Starting with Bible study, it expanded to include reading, writing, arithmetic, and (later) English or French literature, geography, history, and nature study. Originally, little or no attempt was made to encourage the development of technical skills in pupils; and the immediate environment was either ignored or condemned as uneducative, because it was thought to be anti-Christian.

As various African countries approached independence, the Nationalist Movement wished to reorient African education. Nationalists wanted to utilize education to develop Africa's human and material resources. They wanted curricula which could produce practical persons and would reflect African values. Then, in 1961, there was the UNESCO sponsored Addis Ababa Conference of African Ministers of Education.

Lewis (1976. p. 27) has commented:

> When the conference met, only sixteen per cent of the children of school age in Africa were attending school. Yet the African states were already allocating large portions of their national budgets to education. In fact, many of them were spending up to twenty-three per cent of their national budgets for this purpose. The major recommendations of the conference, which were generally accepted by the African governments, were that universal, compulsory and free

22

education, of a minimum of six years, should be provided by 1980, by that year secondary education should be available for three out of every ten children completing primary education, and that efforts should be made to improve the quality of African schools and universities.

The growth of education in the countries of interest since the Addis Ababa Conference has been phenomenal by any standard. Let us for a moment employ the Harbison–Meyer classification system. In this system, developing countries may be placed in three categories, depending on the growth of their educational system and the level of their economic activity. In the first category are those countries where stress is put on the expansion of primary education and the training of a local elite to replace expatriate personnel: second category countries emphasize expansion of secondary education since universal primary education has been seen as attainable. In the third level, the stress is on the nature and quality of higher education. By 1961, all of these countries were at the first stage. We would like to examine the progress that has been made since 1961. The Harbison–Meyer classification system however, deals mostly with quantitative growth. We are also interested in the qualitative growth of the educational services offered to children in these countries.

The chapter will, therefore, review aspects of the development of education at levels below the tertiary level. Starting with pre-school, including the now popular day-care centre activities, it goes through primary and secondary education. It also touches upon special services like school broadcasting, and other radio and television programmes directed to children.

PRE-SCHOOL EDUCATION AND DAY-CARE SERVICES

Pre-school education is mainly private. In all of the countries visited, it is presently handled by individuals and voluntary agencies. In Tanzania for example it is undertaken by women's organizations and religious institutions. Governments also have an essential role. To begin with, there is legislation which enables persons who meet stipulated criteria to establish nursery schools and kindergartens. Registration is usually through the Ministry of Education. Day-care centres are registered either through the Ministry of Health and Social Welfare or the Ministry of Labour and Social Welfare depending on the particular case. These three institutions normally care for children between the ages of two and six years.

Ghana and Tanzania have paid particular attention to the care of children before they are ready to attend formal school. In Ghana the concept of the day-care centres has been successful in gaining acceptance. These centres which care for children under school age of mothers who, because of economic and other activities cannot be with them during part of the day, are becoming widespread in many urban areas and in some rural areas. Provision for the use of the centres is usually made by local authorities, individuals and voluntary agencies. The Department of Social Welfare supervises the activities of the centres, aids in the training of staff, and in the provision of equipment for the implementation of activities. Staff training takes place at the National Day-Care Training Centre, established jointly by the Government of Ghana and UNICEF. It is an important function of the Department of Social Welfare to see that day-care centres provide healthy and wholesome environments, where children receive proper care.

Tanzania, also has paid special attention to day-care centres related to Ujamaa villages. In this connection, the functions of the centres have been specified. They include the provisions that children will be:

(a)   supervised while mothers are engaged in Ujamaa activities;
(b)   taught cleanliness and acceptable social habits;
(c)   taught national ideals;
(d)   prepared for formal education;
(e)   introduced to Kiswahili, if they are from non-Kiswahili speaking ethnic groups.

Aided by financial assistance from UNICEF, the Government of Tanzania has helped to build new centres and has renovated some old ones. In 1972, there were more than 360 day-care centres in Tanzania.

Most African countries have similar programmes, but perhaps not as elaborate as those of Ghana, Tanzania, Ivory Coast, and Senegal. In Ivory Coast, the health of the mother during pregnancy and up to the time of delivery is taken care of by institutions called PMI (Maternal and Infant Protection), under the Ministry of Health. After birth, the mother and infant are encouraged to visit regularly the "social centres" established by the Ministry of Social Services in most large towns. This year, there are thirty-six throughout the country, eight of which are in Abidjan. Mobile teams are able to extend the service to smaller villages, but usually lack the financial support necessary to operate extensively. These social centres provide preventive care, vaccinations for example, as well as nutritional education, continuing the education begun by the PMIs. Day-care centres have proliferated in the main urban centres where rapid social change, effected by industrialization, has led to an increased demand for the institutionalized care of young children. Most of these are managed privately, either by religious organizations or by profit-making private institutions, but the Ministry of Social Services exercises some control over the centres, and is responsible for the training of day-care and nursery-school teachers.

The Ministry of Social Services has established thirty-four government nursery-schools, attached to the "social centres", and plans to extend these services according to the growing demand. It also maintains special schools, or subsidizes private schools for the education of blind, deaf, or otherwise handicapped children, as well as orphanages. This situation is similar to that in Senegal, where a department within the Ministry of Education has been recently created, specifically to handle nursery-schools and pre-schools. With the help of UNICEF, the extension of day-care services to rural areas is being studied, particularly in the province of Casamance, where a traditional system of communal care for very young children is already in practice.

The UNICEF regional office for East Africa in Nairobi has made an effort to develop and improve its contribution to day-care centre activities, particularly emphasizing the needs of pre-school children. This effort has grown out of the realization that much work that was previously done in this field was influenced primarily by imported Western practices, and that this approach was not always suitable for the countries of the region. The results of this approach varied. It was noted that middle-class and upper-class day-care centres in urban areas worked well with staff trained in Western techniques and using Western materials, since most of the children came from homes which had already adopted this style. However, in rural settings, this approach and these practices were often unsuccessful, and sometimes harmful to children, their parents, and teachers. A teacher who must work with fifty children in a village setting, under a shelter with almost no equipment or teaching aid, would find it impossible to initiate the western-type emphasized during her training. With this realization, UNICEF began analysing existing day-care centre (DCC) programmes in African and other countries. The objective was to discover techniques and methods used in day care that were adaptable to the needs of rural Africa.

In 1975 and 1976, two significant activities were undertaken on the behalf of this project. The first was the evaluation of the Kenya day-care centre programme, by the Ministry of Housing and Social Services, in cooperation with the University of Nairobi. The object of the evaluation was to gather information to be used in the revision of the training programme for day-care centre teachers and supervisors, and for the improvement of the standards of rural DCCs by using locally available material. The second was the organization of a workshop in Iringa, Tanzania, "On the use of local material in the development of teaching aids, equipment, and toys for day-care centres", held in cooperation with the Government of Tanzania. Representatives from Tanzania, Kenya, Mozambique, Lesotho, and Ethiopia discussed minimum standards for the organization and administration of day-care services in Africa, the use of indigenous play material, and the production of teaching aids and equipment.

A major recommendation resulting from the Kenya evaluation, as well as the Iringa Workshop, focused on the relationship of day-care services to community programmes. The emphasis of the recommendation was on day-care programmes as an integral part of the total community. Furthermore, stress was placed on the need for close cooperation between day-care services, and education, health and nutrition programmes. The role of parents, as contributors of funds and materials, and as important partners and participants in the day-care service was also emphasized. It was recommended that the training of teachers include self-reliance, initiative, and the ability to work with parents as well as children, to a much greater degree than that given in the present training programme.

PRIMARY EDUCATION

Most of the countries visited by the main contributors of this report had their first commission on education as independent nations immediately before the 1961 UNESCO-sponsored Addis Ababa conference of African Ministers of Education, or shortly thereafter. Nigeria, for example, had the Ashby Commission Report in 1960, and Sierra Leone and Kenya had reports from their national commissions on education in 1963. These reports basically indicated that primary education would be used to establish literacy, impart knowledge and skills, develop the personality of the individual, and produce useful citizens.

Thus, it was the spirit of the Addis Ababa Conference which dominated policy on primary education in these countries during the 1960s. The idea behind the spirit was of making primary education available to as many children as possible. In Nigeria, for example, primary school enrolment increased from 2.8 million in 1961 to 4 million in 1971, for an average annual increase in enrolment of more than four per cent. In Kenya the figures for enrolment are from 891,553 in 1963 to 1,427,589 in 1970, for an average annual increase of more than seven per cent. The average annual rate of enrolment increase in Sierra Leone during the same period was approximately eight per cent. In each case, as in all of the other African countries visited by the main contributors of the report, the rate of increase in primary school enrolment was significantly higher than the population growth rate. However, because the population growth is concentrated in the 0–15 year age group, it is also true that the number of school-age children not enrolled in school remains high.

The initiation of activities in curriculum development at the primary-school level was also begun in the 1960s. A Pan-African curriculum development agency known as the African Education Programme was established in 1961. Its departments were known as the African Mathematics Programme (AMP), the African Primary Science Programme (APSP), and the African Social Studies Programme (ASSP). The African Education Programme appointed itself to the major tasks of developing curricula within its specific departments appropriate for the African child, and of training teachers and curriculum workers in the use and development of such curriculum materials. Materials produced by the AMP, popularly known as Entebbe Mathematics, have had a tremendous impact on the study of primary school mathematics in many African countries. The APSP, which was founded in 1965, and which became more African-oriented as the Science Education Programme for Africa (SEPA) in 1970, has had tremendous impact on education in Africa. This book, in fact, is one of several of its testimonials.

The growth of primary education started in the 1960s and continued in the 1970s at an even faster rate. In Nigeria primary-school enrolment has increased two and half times, from 4 million in 1971 to 10 million in 1977. The average annual increase was twenty-five per cent, due to a substantial increase in primary-school enrolment in 1976/77, when Universal Primary Education (UPE) was introduced. While the enrolment increases in other African countries have not been as dramatic, they have nevertheless been impressive. In Kenya, for example, enrolment more than doubled from

1,427,589 in 1970 to 2,894,617 in 1976. The average annual rate of growth in primary school enrolment being approximately fifteen per cent.

It is in the areas of policy and the quality of the education offered that the distinction between events in the 1960s and in the 1970s may best be made. It is true that the nationalist movement discussed relevant curricula and the incorporation of African values in school experience, and many curriculum development centres sprang up in the 1960s. However, the educational policies and structures of the post-independence era were initially patterned after the educational policies and structures of the preceding colonial governments. Therefore, modifications in curriculum and other aspects of the educational delivery system were token. The bold and imaginative new ventures dictated by the African environment, needed to indicate a modern African approach to education, were not initiated until the 1970s.

It was in that decade that a call was finally made, by Lewis (1967), for connections to be established between African psychologists, curriculum developers, and other educators and teachers, and was taken seriously by African scholars, ministries and institutes of education, and international agencies. In 1968 the Nairobi conference of African Ministers of Education pinpointed certain shortcomings in the educational systems, observed that qualitative improvement appeared to be a prerequisite of quantitative expansion, and suggested recommendations regarding the reform of primary education. It was in the 1970s that the recommendations were being implemented. Also during that decade, the APSP became an important agent for educational innovation in Africa known as the Science Education Programme for Africa (SEPA). Backed by some African governments and scholars, and supported and aided by many international agencies, SEPA has become an extremely effective agent for the development of education in the continent.

The Lagos Conference of Ministers of Education of African member states was the next significant conference. This conference reviewed the trends in education in Africa in the period from 1968 to 1976. It was discovered that most African countries were now devising educational strategies to achieve the cultural, economic, political, and social objectives stipulated in their national policies. The *Final Report* (UNESCO, 1976) states:

> Education is seen as a powerful factor in the establishment of democracy and it is defined in relation to the type of man which it is expected to shape: a man who will be deeply rooted in the cultural traditions of Africa, and in the African environment, aware of his political and civic responsibilities, of his duties to his

family, and prepared to play a useful role as a producer and as a citizen in the economic and social development of the community.

Thus, African countries have started to seek solutions to many of the problems that beset primary education. These include the problem of quantitative expansion (especially given the fact that the rate of population growth is also high), teacher shortages, and physical inadequacies. Another major problem arises from inequitable distribution of opportunities in favour of the urban areas where only a small proportion of the people live. But by far the greatest challenge is devising curricula that will serve the best interest of all primary school pupils. In the majority of these countries and for a significant portion of the population, the completion of primary school will signify the end of formal education.

As was stated in the chapter on social environment, a people's culture consists of the traditions and customs with which they live. In all the countries surveyed, radio broadcasting has become an important channel of information both in urban and in rural areas, while television is becoming rapidly accepted into the urban centres. In answer to both this situation and to the critical problem posed by teacher shortages, and lack of equipment and physical facilities, different governments have begun to use radio and television as important teaching agents. School broadcasting has been established in just about every country visited.

In the Ivory Coast in particular, the educational system has been progressively restructured around a nationwide television programme since 1968. By 1977, the first set of elementary school pupils educated through this system were ready for secondary school. This has inspired a reevaluation of the form and nature of secondary education in that country. The results of a systematic nationwide evaluation of this project and of the impact of the television programme on classroom dynamics should be available within a year. Initial observations suggest that the children involved have become more interested in their education.

SECONDARY EDUCATION

In each state, education has become embedded within the context of the over-all development of that nation; and has thus become intimately related to cultural, economic, and political factors, which have international ramifications. The main objective of secondary education in Africa has been to produce the skilled manpower necessary to aid the development of the various countries. These nations expect that educational development at the secondary and higher levels will effect a new world economic and social order, based on better cooperation among the various peoples of the world and a more equitable distribution of the economic resources available to mankind.

It was indicated earlier that by 1961 all the African countries studied had only just begun to develop primary education. Nevertheless, the recommendation, by the Addis Ababa Conference, that by 1980 approximately thirty per cent of the primary-school enrolment in each country attend secondary school, was generally accepted and vigorously pursued. However, an analysis carried out in 1977 (see Table 1) indicated that observed enrolment for middle Africa (Africa, excluding Algeria, Eygpt, Libya, Morocco, Tunisia, Zimbabwe, and South Africa) fell short of the target enrolment by twelve per cent in 1965, fourteen per cent in 1968 and seventeen per cent in 1971. The trend, therefore, was in the direction of a widening gap between the observed and the target enrolment.

The mean and median of the shortfall during the seven year period from 1965 to 1971, were sixteen per cent and seventeen per cent respectively. An idea of the magnitude of the task which these countries set for themselves at Addis Ababa and of the vigour with which they pursued it may be obtained from the example of Sierra Leone. In 1961 there were 94,218 pupils enrolled in primary school and only 7,777 pupils in secondary schools. That is, only eight per cent of primary school pupils were enrolled in secondary schools.

TABLE 1. SECONDARY SCHOOL
STATISTICS IN MIDDLE AFRICA

| Year | Enrolment | | % |
	Actual	Target	Below Target
1965	1,342,100	1,533,100	13
1966	1,491,430	1,623,450	9
1967	1,623,450	1,971,500	21
1968	1,925,790	2,235,680	14
1969	2,109,320	2,535,260	20
1970	2,446,730	2,975,490	18
1971	2,666,700	3,561,750	17

By 1965 and 1970, this percentage had increased to thirteen per cent and twenty per cent respectively. Given the rapid rate at which primary school enrolment was expanding, achieving the proposed expansion at the secondary-school level was no mean task.

It is relevant, as has been previously indicated, that colonial governments established schools that were alienated from the communities in which they were expected to function. Secondary school was viewed as an institution where a privileged few were collected, housed together, and taught to despise work and their environment. The pupil was brought up to escape from, rather than to learn to gain a measure of control in, his environment. This attitude persists among increasing numbers of pupils entering secondary school. One reason this has been the case is that in some of these countries it is the unexpressed but prevailing notion that a high quality secondary school must be a form of colonial relic, a boarding school.

The new educational policies and structures now being introduced by African countries must view secondary schools as community schools integrated with the community. One outcome of this approach should be that education inevitably becomes linked with work. Another should be that the school in general becomes an instrument for the transformation of the cultural heritage of the people of Africa. And, because of the basic role of language in the culture of a people, learning in African languages must be emphasized at the primary-school level, and the continued study and improvement of these languages must be given priority at the secondary and higher levels of education.

5

OTHER SERVICES

EXTRACURRICULAR

It is public knowledge that the majority of young people in Africa do not receive a formal education for any considerable amount of time. Those young people will form the majority of the population which as citizens will be expected to perform basic services for each country, such as food production. The school is unable to fulfil its task of educating the large numbers of young people, who should be educated with regard to the nature of their environment.

The education of people who are out of school can take several forms. In most countries there exist non-formal educational projects which strive for the educational developments of youth utilizing apprenticeship programmes of the old order. Some of these are private enterprises, but governments in some countries, through various ministries, have or are developing such projects, thereby providing services which will aid the development of these young people.

Some of these services are rendered through the assistance of particular agencies. We cite the work of the Science Education Programme for Africa (SEPA) in relation to these non-formal educational services. A programme known as the Out-of-School Youth (OOSY) Programme was initiated to reach young people in their communities and to give them opportunity to learn problem-solving skills, habits of thought attuned to change, and effective communication skills, by giving them an education based on livelihood activities in their immediate environment. SEPA was aware of the existence of these developmental projects, so initially the OOSY Programme studied existing projects, with the intention of using the successes of these projects to create a model to be applied in the establishment of other non-formal educational projects.

The projects studied include the following:

(1) The Fishing and Boat-Building Apprenticeship Project at Tombo (Sierra Leone). This is a viable and useful project in a community whose main occupation is fishing. Boats are built or repaired. Apprentices become wards of the master craftsman, to be "redeemed" after their apprenticeship is over.

SEPA's entry into the project has resulted in the creation of plans for improvement of the training procedures, the design of the boats, and the fishing gear.

(2) The Integrated Rural Workshop at Winneba (Ghana) specializes in the education of blacksmiths who are illiterate. Blacksmiths working individually in isolated villages were brought together for training in metal work — the production of hoes, files, wheelbarrows, safety locks, coal pots, planes, and a variety of other items — as well as in the repair and improvisation of farm equipment.

The current group of learners are blacksmiths who are learning fine details of the trade and a few scientific methods. They also learn to improvise and make tools from discarded scrap metal (from broken saws for example) and the use of palm kernel shells for fuel in the forge.

(3) Another example of rural development occurred in Lesotho in the 1950s. Father Benua encouraged a local lady, Mrs M'Qato, at the village of Ha Tsulcane, Lesotho, to teach other ladies the craft of making Sotho hats. These ladies later formed a hat-making cooperative, selling hats to curioshops and tourists.

(4) The Betty Carew Women's Training Centre (Sierra Leone) was established a little over a year ago to bring women together. Their objectives are to participate in mutual learning, to revive and improve upon women's traditional skills, including child care and nutrition, to enhance women's self-reliance and self-image, and to alleviate the trend toward depression sweeping the rural communities. The skills they learn include making hand bags, purses, bracelets, belts, necklaces, earrings, table mats, and dresses for children and adults. Plans for the inclusion of tie-dyeing are under way. All of these products are in demand, and are currently in style.

(5) The Special Rural Development Project at the Vihiga and Hamisi Divisions of the Kakamega District (Kenya) had been undertaken to identify

and concentrate on critical development gaps and congestion, to establish procedures and techniques for self-generated rural development elsewhere in the country, and to improve the training of extension workers. The project has not been considered successful and, consequently, SEPA has started an experimental programme for out-of-school youth, utilizing the SEPA approach.

(6) The Kalawa Community Project is centred around tailoring as the area is arid and unsuitable for commercial agricultural activity. The project has been started by the initiative of a SEPA specialist in Kenya. After a survey of the community, it was learned that the community had too many primary-school leavers to be absorbed by the one existing secondary school. The community therefore decided upon tailoring as a useful alternative enterprise for the young people.

(7) In the Awka community (in Nigeria), two primary occupations are farming and blacksmithing. The practice had been to apprentice children to blacksmiths but, with the introduction of universal primary education, a change in the system of apprenticeship is essential, otherwise the loss of interest in blacksmithing will approach crisis proportions. SEPA organizers plan to revive interest by selecting elementary-school children for training in blacksmithing after school, as well as attempting to incorporate the apprenticeship into the formal school programme.

Blacksmiths in the community will be organized into a cooperative and the children will spend about two hours a day studying under master craftsmen. Upon completion of primary school, some of the children could begin the trade full-time, while others could continue part-time, after school hours. As the project progresses, it will include carving, because Awka carvings are unique, and yield quick dividends. The project will encourage the use of local materials, and will also investigate traditional systems of education in the Awka area.

Subsequent activities of the OOSY programme will handle the production of materials, in order to facilitate change agents in their endeavour to aid educational development projects, using the research materials obtained in the preparation of the case studies cited above. In this material development phase five manuals have been prepared. *Needs Assessment* deals with tasks, approaches and procedures that constitute identifying the needs of a community, and determining the type of project to be undertaken by that community; the human and material resources and the processes necessary as inputs to that particular project; the need of the external and internal change agents to understand the community, the components necessary to establish and run a successful development project, and the needs of the learners in such a project.

There are three trial manuals based on the experiences of three trainers, *'Strategies for Skills Transfer'*. The skills to be transferred include blacksmithing, tailoring, and macrame. The purpose of these manuals is to collect the experience of these master craftsmen and to utilize it as a tool to enable replication of the type of training they give to their learners. These manuals cover such topics as getting started, familiarization, making simple objects, mastering the art, evaluation, and management techniques.

The other material is a monograph dealing with the development of the Kenya case study to illustrate SEPA's recommended approach to out-of-school youth development projects. The monograph is divided into sections dealing with:

(a) A description of SEPA's general approach to education.
(b) The model, an appropriate tool for establishing and running projects for the education of out-of-school youth.
(c) An illustrative case, in Kenya, where the tool has been utilized in an existing project.
(d) Another illustration showing the use of the model in actually starting a new project.

To complete the monograph there is an additional section on its broad social and economic implications.

The manuals are available for use by individuals, governments, and agencies who are concerned with the development of youths in non-formal educational systems.

BASIC EDUCATION RESOURCES CENTRE FOR EASTERN AFRICA

Governments throughout Africa are intent upon universalizing education, but they are even more preoccupied with dispensing the sort of education which prepares the citizens for life in their specific socioeconomic and cultural environment. Every educational reform that has occurred in these countries since independence has had these two objectives.

In undertaking these reforms, which is a never-ending process necessitated by change and progress, the countries of Africa, especially those with close geographical and cultural affinities, have increasingly sought to compare notes and derive benefit from mutual experience. This trend has brought about a considerable number of meetings, at regional and subregional levels, inter-country visits by administrative and professional educational personnel, and a general interest in the educational progress in neighbouring countries.

Basic education is one area in which a great deal of interaction has taken place, especially since the first Seminars on Basic Education in Eastern Africa took place in Nairobi in July and October 1974. These seminars were held under the auspices of the UNESCO/UNICEF Cooperation Programme, which has strongly supported the efforts of the countries in the Eastern African region in their endeavours to universalize basic education since then.

The Basic Education Resources Centre for Eastern Africa (BERC) was founded at Kenyatta University College, Nairobi, in September, 1975, intending to facilitate this sort of interaction. Its sole purpose is to promote an exchange of ideas and experiences among Eastern African countries, in the area of basic education.

The term basic education is used to mean an education which promotes the attitudes, values, knowledge, and skills required by any citizen to lead a respectable human life and be an asset to society.

Basic education is concerned with fostering every aspect of human development, individual and social — the economic, the physical, the emotional, the intellectual, the moral, and the aesthetic. It is not an end in itself, nor is it oriented towards further formal studies. It is an education for life in the immediate future, and at the same time, the beginning of life-long education. This should enable a person to live a life free from misery, hunger, unwarranted disease, undue poverty, and degrading ignorance.

Participants in the Seminar on Teacher Education for Basic Education, held in Tanzania and Burundi in November 1977, neatly summarized the over-all objectives of any basic education programme in the following terms:

> Basic education, in addition to teaching reading, writing and arithmetic should promote: a scientific and technical knowledge of the environment; a desire to improve it and the ability to do so communally; positive attitudes towards self as a human person, others, work and country; the cultural, moral and civic values of the community.

BERC is essentially a service; it is intended to act as a regional information, research and training centre for Eastern Africa, to constitute a forum for sharing ideas and experiences in the area of basic education, and to form the nucleus of a network of basic education units spread throughout the region.

YOUTH CLUBS AND YOUTH ORGANIZATIONS

It was pointed out in an earlier section that one of the results of the rapid increase of population in many African countries is the overrepresentation of the age group of 15 years and below in the total population. One consequence has been that not many African governments are able to provide enough schools for the formal education of this young population. Moreover, the large number of drop-outs from the formal school system has forced many governments to create solutions for dealing with out-of-school youth. One such solution is the creation of youth clubs and other youth organizations.

Youth clubs have become very important factors in community and national development. They are active in a variety of areas, interest areas including promotion of educational policies, social, cultural, and sporting activities, and agriculture. In some countries, they also provide a good recruiting ground for the security forces of the countries.

Usually there are large numbers of these clubs in each country. For example, there were at least thirty-two such clubs in Liberia early last year, all organized by a powerful national association known as the Federation of Liberian Youth. In Sierra Leone, there were two hundred and fifty-two clubs last year.

In other African countries, ministries of Social Welfare or Rural Development have sections responsible for out-of-school youth, while ministries of Education are directly responsible for school children.

RECREATIONAL SERVICES

In several African countries, considerable amounts of effort, time, and money go into the organization of sports and other recreational services. This is a result of the realization that these services are essential for a number of reasons. They promote health and fitness in the participants. They keep the participants occupied for a considerable amount of time; time which otherwise might be used in activities destructive to the community interests.

In villages and schools, several competitions are held in such sports as football, lawn tennis, table tennis, athletics, volley ball, basket ball, and hockey.

In Nigeria, such competitions would be organized by the government and schools. The competitions would start at local government level, then move on to the state government level, and finally to the national level. In schools, they start at the inter-house level within the schools themselves, move on to inter-school level, regional level, and then to state level.

EDUCATIONAL RADIO AND TELEVISION

Realizing the critical problems posed by teacher shortages, lack of equipment and physical facilities, various African governments have resorted to the use of television and radio in an attempt to reach a wide audience, and to provide more effective teaching.

In addition to the educational television programmes utilized in the Ivory Coast, educational radio broadcasts are also used, mainly for primary schools. In this area in particular the teachers are in need of specialized help.

One problem posed by the use of radio and television is the very high cost, not only of installing the equipment, buying radio and television sets, but of keeping the equipment in working condition. Whether the radio and television programmes are used creatively by the classroom teacher probably depends very much on his training and initiative.

6

CHILD DEVELOPMENT
(1) PSYCHOMOTOR AND AFFECTIVE DEVELOPMENT

IMPROVING the quality of life, developing the maximum potential of each individual, and fostering a balanced interaction with the environment are worthwhile goals for each individual throughout the life span; they are priorities during childhood. "It is now being increasingly recognized that the policies and programmes developing countries adopt for their children can make a significant contribution to all other national long-term development activities" (UNICEF, 1977). And, childhood is the period in the life-cycle in which investments are likely to bring maximum returns. This is well recognized, and explains why most developing countries spend more than twenty per cent of their annual budgets on education. This tremendous effort can be made even more profitable if it is based on a thorough knowledge of the characteristics of child development and of the environmental factors affecting it.

Infancy is the period of childhood in which the foundations for future development are laid. It is also the period during which the child is most dependent, most vulnerable to harmful aspects of the environment, and needs the most protection from various diseases, hazards, and handicaps. It is therefore important to consider in some detail what is known about the development of the African infant in relation to his environment.

Infancy has been a privileged area of study in psychology and paediatrics. Many careful studies have been carried out on the physical growth of infants, on neurological maturation during the first months of life, on inborn reflex mechanisms and behaviours, and the progressive emergence of more and more complex behaviour patterns. Early studies have been mainly descriptive, and have developed quantitative scales to assess infant development; recent studies have become more experimental, and are more

39

likely to disentangle the complex interaction between maturation and environment. This study, however, is not the place in which to review this vast area of knowledge.

Most of this work has been carried out in Western, industrialized countries – therefore, on a very limited sample of the world population. Although it is not unreasonable to assume that many aspects of development during infancy are universal, it is also obvious that environmental factors influence the child's development from the moment of birth, and even before, and produce sufficient variation to preclude any simple generalization from Western findings. Some research has been carried out on development during infancy in non-Western cultures, particularly in Africa, but there are still many gaps in our knowledge. Reviews of this cross-cultural work have been provided by Werner (1972), Munroe and Munroe (1975), Rebelsky and Daniel (1976) and others, the most complete and methodologically thorough being a handbook chapter by Super (in preparation). Dague (1970a), Zempléni and Zempléni (1972), and Wober (1975) deal with infancy and weaning in Africa specifically, and Erny (1972a) provides an ethnological account of traditional customs, attitudes and beliefs concerning pregnancy, birth and infant development in sub-Saharan Africa.

If Western findings cannot be extended to Africa without careful experimentation, data from one part of Africa cannot necessarily be generalized to the whole continent. There are so many different forms of social organization, and such a variety in the physical and cultural environments, that it is hardly possible to speak of "the" African child. However there certainly are some cultural and psychological similarities in the traditional outlook on childhood, and common or similar changes and problems brought about by industrialization and urbanization. Any general statement on the African child in the African environment is clearly impossible, and we should keep this in mind while reading the following, necessarily oversimplified, account of infancy in the African environment.

PREGNANCY AND NEONATAL DEVELOPMENTAL STATUS

The positive attitude of African women towards pregnancy and childbirth, and the placement of high value on having children are common generalizations. A woman's status is determined primarily by her fertility. Given this positive outlook, pregnancy is usually a happy and relaxed period, during which the woman continues to be active, and the absence of anxiety is likely to have a positive effect on the infant's development (Ferreira, 1960; Davids *et al.*, 1963; Ottinger and Simmons, 1964). Some fears may occur, however, regarding the health of the mother during pregnancy, the difficulty of child-birth, and especially the high infant mortality; these are accompanied by beliefs and practices which may alleviate anxieties. For example, many African women observe certain social and food taboos during pregnancy (which are not always nutritionally advantageous), newborns are not named immediately, and are not given the burial ceremony reserved for older children. Generally speaking, though, it can be said that African children arrive into a basically welcoming world and have a good start in life.

Several studies have attempted to assess the developmental status of African newborns, among which is a much quoted report by Geber and Dean (1957) on the precocity of neonates in Kampala, which seems to have been widely accepted despite serious methodological shortcomings. The authors studied 107 infants between birth and 8 days old, all of birthweight above 2500 g and having normal delivery, using a routine neurological examination. They found that most behaviours were advanced over Euro-American norms by about four to six weeks, some even six to eight weeks (head control for example). It should be noted that developmental status at birth is not deter-mined entirely by heredity, because environmental influences occur during pregnancy.

Warren and Parkin (1974), also working in Kampala, failed to replicate several of Geber and Dean's findings in a much more carefully controlled and reported study, and studies by Griffiths (1969) in South Africa, by Konner (1972) in Botswana, and by Super and Brazelton in Kenya (Super, in preparation) basically show no difference in neurological development between African and Euro-American norms. Vouilloux (1959) on the other hand confirmed the precocity in Douala (Cameroun).

Neonatal precocity is therefore far from confirmed, and will probably remain a controversial issue for some time to come, notably because of the methodological difficulties linked to the developmental assessment of newborns. (Super, in preparation).

One of these difficulties deals with the definition of prematurity. The birthweight of infants of African ancestry is usually below 3000 g (Werner, 1972) so that the limit below which an infant is judged premature ought to be lowered to 2100 g (Super, in preparation) or even 1800 g (Wober, 1975) instead of the usual limit of 2500 g. Also determining the length of the gestation period with precision is often impossible.

Reinhardt, Gautier and Reinhardt (in press) used the clinical assessment of neurological or physical maturity (Dubowitz *et al.*, 1970) in a study of lower class urban mothers and their newborn babies. He found twenty-three per cent prematurity. This high proportion of risk cases is related to the poor health of the mothers: seventy-five per cent seemed to suffer from moderate malnutrition, most were anaemic, forty per cent presented malaria infection, and in more than half of these cases, parasites were also found in the umbilical cord. (Reinhardt, Gautier and Reinhardt, in press). The greatest proportion of high risk cases was found in first-born children of very young mothers who have become pregnant before achieving full growth. Several closely spaced births and poor nutrition may similarly cause a "physiologically inadequate intrauterine environment" which has a negative effect on developmental status (Brazelton, Koslowski and Tronik, 1976, as cited in Super, in preparation).

PHYSICAL DEVELOPMENT

Basically, the factors associated with the physical development of the child can be classified into primary and secondary ones. The primary factors include heredity, nutrition, the condition of the mother during pregnancy, ill health, the physical environment, aspects of the social environment, emotional and other psychological factors during the early stages of life. The secondary factors include family size, the position of the particular child in the family, the socioeconomic status and educational level of the parents, the spacing of children, and the attitude of the particular society to children.

Thus, children of the same age in different societies or within the same society will be at different levels of physical development depending on these prenatal and postnatal factors. The role of heredity, it would appear, is to provide the potential for growth. The extent to which this potential is utilized is determined by the other factors, usually in their interrelationships and interactions. For instance, physical development is known to take place at a slower pace during the rainy season than during the dry season. As Durojaiye (1976) has observed:

In some countries in Africa poor growth in children is noticed in the rainy season, and increases in both weight and height are often good in the dry season. Poor growth in the rainy season may be due to inadequate food supply and to increased risk of catching the infectious diseases transmitted by insects. Maternal care also suffers during this season as mothers are out in the field helping their husbands cultivate the land. Sleep also suffers because of insects and high humidity.

Such seasonal variations have been noted also in a longitudinal study by Dasen *et al.* (1978): weight is very sensitive to fluctuations in food supply and disease, whereas other anthropometric measures (such as height, head to chest, and arm circumference) reflect long-term effects of environmental conditions.

Several studies covering physical development during the pre-school period have been carried out in West Africa. They include investigations in Sierra Leone, Senegal, Nigeria, Ghana, and the Gambia. The general pattern of growth observed is that elite homes in the cities encourage good growth, while rural homes and homes in urban slums have given rise to slow growth. In particular, in her longitudinal study at Ibadan, Nigeria, Janes (cited in Durojaiye, 1976) discovered that the average differences in height between children from elite and lower class Oje homes were significant by the age of four weeks for boys and three months for girls. By the age of four years the average difference in weight was 2.59 kg. What is more, the children from elite homes would continue to grow faster. By the age of seven, the average difference in height was 9.4 cm and in weight 4.47 kg.

Weight and height data for African infants and children are reported by Morley (1973) and Uka for Nigeria, Thompson − Clewry for Sierra Leone, the latter study using well nourished children, which is necessary if the results are to be considered as "norms".

Morley (1973) has pointed out the importance of the use of the weight curve in paediatrics and preventive infant care, and he presents illustrations demonstrating the use of the health chart in an infant clinic by minimally trained paramedical staff. It is not actually necessary to have local growth norms to use such charts, as regular weight gain is more important than the absolute position of the weight curve on the chart.

PSYCHOMOTOR DEVELOPMENT

Psychological development during the first three years of life has usually been studied through so-called "baby-tests" (Bayley, 1969; Griffiths, 1970; Brunet and Lézine, 1971) based on the work of Gesell and Amatruda (1947). These are composite scales or schedules of developmental landmarks such as motor head control, eye–hand coordination, sitting, standing, walking, etc. Most tests also include items or sub-scales to measure behaviour which is not purely motor: smiling, imitation, frown discrimination, language, etc. Cross-cultural studies using these baby-tests have been reviewed by Werner (1972) and Super (in preparation). The African evidence has been more specifically studied by Warren (1972), Dasen (1974) and Wober (1975).

The usual findings are of a marked precocity compared to Euro-American norms in psychomotor development in the first year of life. The samples were reared in traditional, pre-industrial communities. They shared cultural and environmental characteristics such as membership of an extended family with many caretakers, breast feeding on demand, constant tactile stimulation by the body of the caretaker (via back-carrying), participation in adult activities and lack of restrictive clothing (Werner, 1972). Despite some methodological difficulties (Warren, 1972), this precocity, attributed pre-dominantly or exclusively to environmental factors, is confirmed by studies in Botswana, Cameroon, Guinea, Ivory Coast, Kenya, Madagascar, Nigeria, Senegal, Tanzania, Uganda, and Zambia, and there is strong evidence for generalizing these findings for all of Africa. Conflicting results are found in the study of South Africa; one study reported precocity and two studies found no difference. As Wober (1975) points out, studies emerging from South Africa must be viewed with caution because the prevailing socio-political conditions may adversely affect both the psychological development and the experimental situation in which it is assessed.

Another common finding is the later decline of psychomotor scores, beginning either in the second half of the first year or in the second year. The sharpest early decline is found among infants in the urban slums whose period of breast feeding is consistently shorter than that of rural communities (Werner, 1972). The decline is generally attributed to malnutrition and to the nutritional and psychological ill-effects of sudden weaning. Both the phenomenon of the decline and its explanation, are questionable. As Dasen (1974) has pointed out, the decline could be at least partly a result of the measuring scale (the method of calculating a developmental-quotient and increasing cultural bias with age) or of the testing situation (such as increased emotional reactions to strangers and strange situations in the second year). Attributing the decline to malnutrition and sudden weaning is pure speculation; although it may be correct, no study has clearly demonstrated this relationship.

Psychomotor precocity has been attributed to the intimate mother–infant relationship and the beneficial climate of security, and to several aspects of infant care, back-carrying for example, or systematic motor stimulation such as massaging and other vigorous handling of the infants. However, the variables are notoriously confounded or "packaged" (Whiting, 1976). The hypothesized independent variables usually occur together, and can not therefore be linked individually to the dependent variables, the baby-test scores, which are also composites of diverse aspects of behaviour.

A theoretically more sophisticated approach has led Super in 1973 to question the idea of an over-all precocity in African infants. Instead of using the scores on baby-tests, Super examined specific behaviours. African infants, according to this approach, are relatively advanced in behaviours which (1) they are specifically taught, and (2) they can practise often. These include, most prominently, sitting and walking. African babies achieve other milestones at the same time or later than infants from other cultures, again depending on specific environmental encouragement and support. Prone behaviours, such as lifting the head, turning over, crawling, for example, are not particularly valued or encouraged, and there is little opportunity for the babies to practise them, since they are rarely set down while awake (Super, in preparation).

This environmental argument for "limited" African infant precocity, linked to specific infant training practices, is upheld by a recent study in Kenya by Kilbride (1977). Earlier research by Kilbride and Kilbride (1974, 1975) in Uganda had demonstrated that sociability was highly valued in some African groups, such as the Baganda, where social status is achieved rather than ascribed. Baganda infants were advanced on six of eleven "sociability" items of the Bayley scale, particularly, responding to a person's voice, reacting to the disappearance of a person's face, and smiling, vocalizing and responding playfully to a mirror image. Previous research using the baby-test approach had also found some precocity in language and sociability, although not as consistently as in psychomotor development.

Further support for environmental influence comes from intracultural comparisons of samples from different socioeconomic backgrounds. In Western studies, social class differences are shown to affect psychological development consistently only after the onset of language, but the sporadic effects which have been found in infancy usually favour the higher socio-economic group. In Africa, this is not the case. The development of infants from more "westernized", urban, middle-class (sometimes called "elite") samples is usually not as accelerated as that of traditionally reared, rural infants, although their scores are still superior to those of Western infants, and no decline is reported in later months. This is explained by the lower value attached to pregnancy and childbirth, higher anxiety during pregnancy, less frequent and shorter breast feeding, more progressive weaning, and less stimulation available (attributed to development in a nuclear family, sleeping alone in a cot or crib, absence of back-carrying, etc.). However, again, these variables are "packaged", and the relevant aspects of infant care are usually not measured directly. This may explain some of the conflicting results, produced by studies in Nigeria, Uganda, and Kenya, where no social-class effects were found, or where the opposite relationship is reported (Super, in preparation).

EMOTIONAL DEVELOPMENT

The development of the child always occurs in a physical, social and cultural environment; it is inseparable from this context. In a similar manner, various aspects of this development are linked, mutually interdependent, or inseparable; it is only for the purpose of study that the behavioural sciences tend to establish separate categories. Thus, when we speak of the intellectual development of the child, we should bear in mind that we are carrying out a dissection; in fact intellectual development and social and emotional development are interdependent.

The clear separation of various aspects of development, and an emphasis on cognitive functions, is typical of the experimental method, and characterizes much of the psychological research in Anglophone countries. In the French-speaking world, where psychology tends to remain linked with philosophy, a more global approach is often preferred and as much emphasis is given to affective development as to psychopathology. Thus, a style very common in Francophone Africa is the ethno-psychological approach typified by the early work in Zaire of Knappen (1962), followed by Erny (1972a, 1972b), and recently by a large number of studies emerging from the National University of Zaire, as well as other Francophone countries (Zagre,

1976, in Upper-Volta). Through participant observation or an analysis of the ethnographic literature, these authors describe the development of the child in its traditional context. They utilize a global approach in which the social, cultural, affective, and intellectual aspects are intimately linked. The emphasis is based on the "modal" or "basal" personality of the child in a developmental perspective.

Another, more theoretical approach stems from Western psychoanalysis, and has given rise to the "culture and personality" school, using either anthropological methods of case studies, world-wide cross-cultural comparisons, or psychological projective tests. Freudian hypotheses have of course received most of the attention. This approach, with its achievements and methodological difficulties, has been described by Le Vine (1973) and Kline (1977), and is covered in the relevant sections of the introductory texts and readers by Price-Williams (1969, 1975), Dague, (1970a), Wober (1975) and Serpell (1976).

Still another approach to emotional development, closer to the methods of psychology, deals with values, aspirations, motives, and attitudes, as well as personality. The African material is adequately dealt with by Wober (1975), although a large part of that research involves adults rather than children. Dakar (Senegal) has been the centre for research in psychopathology and psychiatry of the child, as well as the adult, primarily under the direction of Professor Collomb. A complete and annotated bibliography of that work is being prepared for the journal *Psychopathologie Africaine* (edited and published in Dakar by the Société de Psychopathologie et d'Hygiène Mentale) by R. Collignon.

It would be beyond the scope of this report to go into the details of all these aspects of emotional development, especially since this could not be done without an extensive methodological critique. As an illustration of this area of psychological development, let us examine an event of infancy believed to have an important effect on the development of the African child and on his later personality. That event is sudden and harsh weaning, said to be typical throughout most of Africa. This is a good example, as in various theoretical formulations (psychoanalysis, social-learning theory, and ethology) infantile experiences are said to be critical in the development of the affective system (Munroe and Munroe, 1975); furthermore, this example illustrates the controversies which are inevitable in an area where experimental verification is often replaced by philosophical speculation.

In traditional societies, weaning usually occurs between 12 and 18 months, sometimes between 18 and 24 months, and occasionally even later; weaning in the first year of life is rather unusual, except in Westernized, urban groups. The weaning process has been described as sudden and harsh: the child is suddenly refused the breast, often rendered unpalatable by bitter substances) and must adjust to inappropriate adult food. The child is no longer allowed to sleep with his mother, he is sometimes given to a relative to be cared for, and in general, the psychological atmosphere of indulgence, loving care and warmth, changes to one in which respect and obedience are expected.

Because of the sudden change in the emotional environment of the child, weaning has been described as a trauma, a psychological shock, a "millstone, not just a milestone" (Wober, 1975), and its effects are said to be damaging to the child's healthy development. Sudden weaning is supposed to produce a syndrome of depression and depossession (Dague, 1970a), and is said to be the cause of malnutrition and deceleration of psychomotor development. Psychoanalysts have seen this early trauma as a blow to the development of a secure personality, and referred to it in explanation of the African adult personality, which they described as "passive, submissive and resigned". Erny (1972b) interprets the harsh weaning as the African equivalent of the Oedipus complex:

> Pour des raisons extérieures et qui ne tiennent donc pas à la maturation psycho-logique spontanée de l'enfant, le milieu décide qu'il est temps d'arracher celui-ci à sa mère. L'enfant ayant vécu jusque-là dans un rapport de quasi-symbiose avec la mère se trouve brusquement jeté dans le néant relationnel, un monde de solitude, froid et vide. . . . Le mouvement, enduré passivement, par lequel l'enfant se trouve éjecté hors de l'univers maternel, suit un symbolisme à dominante orale-négative: l'éloignement de la mère se présente sous forme de l'interdiction d'une nourriture. Le sevrage, frustration brutale et non preparée, tend à figer l'enfant dans une attitude régressive de nostalgie . . . Cette régression a pour effet et pour but d'enfoncer l'enfant dans un sentiment de dépendance qui seul permet au système familial traditionnel de subsister et de se perpétuer.*

* For external reasons which have nothing to do with the spontaneous psychological development of the child, the environment decides that it is time to wrench the child from the mother. The child, who has lived up to then in a quasi-symbiotic state with the mother is suddenly thrown into a relational vacuum, a world of loneliness, cold and empty . . . . The dynamic through which the child is ejected from the mother's world, and which the child endures passively, follows a symbolism with a negative-oral dominance: the separation from the mother occurs as a food prohibition. The brutal and unexpected frustration of weaning tends to restrict the child to a regressive attitude of nostalgia . . . . The regression has as goal and effect to force the child into a feeling of dependence which is necessary to allow the traditional family system to subsist.

However, the weaning process is not viewed by all in this manner. There is disagreement regarding both the description of the process and its supposed effects. To begin with, weaning is not always harsh; infants are often given adult foods as a supplement to breast feeding at the age of 4 to 6 months, and there is a gradual transition from mother's milk to other foods (Ainsworth, 1967, Zempléni-Rabain, 1968). The infant is introduced at a very early age to social exchanges and to sharing with siblings and age-mates; he is therefore socially integrated before the maternal "rejection" occurs (Zempléni-Rabain, 1968) and he is not left as isolated as has been claimed. There is probably great variation in weaning practices across Africa, traditionally, and recently, under the influence of modernization. This variability logically precludes any generalization of the effects on an "African personality".

The effects of weaning, then, may be much less drastic than has been claimed. Albino and Thompson (1956), have carried out one of the few longitudinal studies covering the weaning period, and have found that weaning plays a dynamic and creative role in the child's development. During the weaning days, the children were indeed negativistic, aggressive, and described as "naughty" by their mothers. However, "most children in the sample suddenly developed forms of behaviour normally expected only of older children, such as helping in household tasks, an increased facility in speech and a greater independence of the support of adults" (p. 186). While the negative behaviour disappears rapidly, the positive aspects remain permanently. Late weaning, therefore, "far from being a merely disorganizing experience . . . , is also a socializing, and maturing influence" (p. 195). If weaning occurs early in life, the disorganization of behaviour is more serious and tends to outweigh any socializing influences.

MALNUTRITION AND ITS EFFECTS ON PSYCHOLOGICAL DEVELOPMENT

We conclude this chapter with a brief reference to malnutrition and its possible effects on development. There is no proof of a link between weaning and supposed deceleration in psychomotor development, except that they have been observed to occur at about the same age — a very tenuous base for a causal inference, even if malnutrition is seen as an intervening variable. Signs of malnutrition, however, occur usually before the actual weaning, and the nutritional status may even improve after weaning (Sieye, 1975). The question of malnutrition and its effects on psychological development is therefore an important one, and deserves special attention.

Thus far in our discussion of infancy in Africa, we have found that the social and emotional environments, and most of the traditional child-rearing practices, especially in the first year of life, have positive effects on the infant's development, with the possible, but controversial, exception of sudden weaning. While the psychosocial development of the African infant is well provided for, his health is less adequately protected (Morley, 1973). Among the many health hazards in the African environment, (though wide variation exists across the continent) malnutrition, associated with parasitic infectious diseases is the greatest cause of infant death. In most African countries, even today, between twenty-five and fifty per cent of the children die before the age of 5 years. Yet only a very small proportion of these deaths is ineluctable; most could be prevented by a combination of the development and management of water resources, sanitary education and preventive medicine. The problem is obviously linked to economic development and the proper distribution of resources (Morley, 1973), and only an integrated development plan, paying special attention to the mother/child/youth group as advocated by UNICEF, can solve it.

Malnutrition is a complex phenomenon. It is obviously, but only partially, connected with food intake, in particular to the low protein and calorie content of common staple foods such as yam, cassava and plantain banana. Fortunately, most African infants are still breast-fed. Breast-feeding is not only the most convenient and sanitary method of infant feeding, it also has important social and psychological ramifications. Human milk is perfectly adapted to the human infant; in addition to nutrients, it provides antibodies which protect the child against infection. A recent study by Lauber and Reinhardt (in press), has shown that the quality of breast milk in a sample of women of the rural Ivory Coast is comparable to that of women of Western countries. Also that the quality remains stable over twenty-three months of breast feeding. The nutritional status of the infant is highly connected to the nutritional status of the mother, indicating the importance of the mother's health and nutrition during pregnancy and lactation. This study, as well as others (Gabbud et al., 1975; Sieye, 1975; Dasen, Inhelder et al., 1978), shows that the nutritional status of the infants tends to decline after the age of 5–10 months. This is probably because the breast milk, although stable in quality, is no longer sufficient in quantity, and the nutritional value of the supplementary foods introduced at that time (such as boiled yams) is insufficient. Finding a locally produced supplemental feeding and weaning food that is inexpensive, yet contains a high protein content, is a priority problem in most of the Third World.

Unfortunately, because of the pressure of urbanization and social change, and the deleterious and unethical publicity of some companies marketing commercial infant foods, bottle feeding has become more widespread. In urban areas, mothers may turn to bottle-feeding as a result of their employment. There also exists a concurrent change in attitudes: the breast becomes a sex symbol rather than a source of nourishment, bottle-feeding is seen as "modern" and therefore desirable; and artificial feeding is advertised and believed to give "power and strength". While commercial baby foods, such as powdered milk, are not themselves harmful, there are two major problems associated with bottle-feeding:

(1) The vast majority of the population, given the present economic situation in Africa, cannot afford it. The problem that many mothers who start bottle-feeding do not realize, is that the quantity of powdered milk needed increases rapidly with the age of the infant, and becomes a major drain on limited resources. It the proper amount is not administered, malnutrition results.

(2) Bottle-feeding requires proper sanitary precautions, otherwise it becomes a health hazard. The usual conditions of water supply and cooking facilities in Africa, and lack of sanitary education, simply do not meet these standards.

Until integrated development and education programmes can change this situation, bottle-feeding is not a suitable nutritional supplement to, nor replacement for, breast-feeding. Governments should take the necessary measures to protect the populations in this respect, through severe control over the prices of commercial infant foods and over the marketing practices associated with their distribution.

Prolonged breast-feeding in the second year without proper food supplementation can also lead to moderate malnutrition (Sieye, 1975), and the adult food given after weaning is often inadequate and insufficient. In some African cultures, the custom is to serve food in accordance to hierarchical social status, first the adult males, then the adult women and the older children, and finally the younger children are fed. Although there is value placed on sharing, the social organization of the family meal means that the youngest children, who would need proteins the most, usually get the least (Dasen, Inhelder *et al.*, 1978).

Malnutrition, however, is associated not only with poor food intake, but also with infectious diseases such as malaria, measles, and chronic intestinal parasites. Moderate malnutrition lowers the organism's resistance to these diseases, which in turn upsets metabolic equilibrium which tends to be at the lower limits of normal values (e.g. Gabbud *et al.*, 1975; Dasen, Inhelder *et al.*, 1978) and precipitates the child into severe malnutrition.

It is often claimed that malnutrition affects the psychological development of the child and prevents him from attaining his maximum potential; if that is true, the implications for the economic and industrial development in countries in which malnutrition is endemic are obviously important.

A large amount of research has been attempted in order to substantiate this claim. However, the area is beset with methodological difficulties, and the results are not clear. It is difficult to extrapolate from controlled animal studies to human development, and studies with human populations are usually confused by variables, such as socioeconomic conditions. Although none of the studies is methodologically perfect, the accumulation of the results points to the following conclusions: severe[†] malnutrition (marasma and kwashiorkor) has a permanent effect on intellectual development if it occurs early in life (Cravioto and Robles, 1965; Winick, 1969; Hertzig *et al.*, 1972: Stock and Smythe, 1967) and if it is associated with periods of chronic undernutrition (Hoorweg, 1976). The effects are not permanent if it occurs later in life (after two years of age), and if there is only one incidence of acute malnutrition. The effect on psychological development could occur in two different ways:

(1) It could affect brain maturation directly, especially during the brain's maximum growth period.

(2) It could affect intellectual development indirectly, through reduced stimulation and activity.

[†] Protein-energy malnutrition can be labelled "severe" if, without proper medical treatment, it leads to death; the common syndromes are marasma and kwashiorkor, and combinations of these. "Moderate" malnutrition usually does not lead to hospitilization or death, unless associated with a disease; there are no obvious clinical signs, but it can be detected by anthropometric methods (Jelliffe, 1966: Wellcome, 1970: Waterlow, 1972: McLaren and Read, 1972).

Chronic moderate malnutrition also has an effect on early psychological development: effects have been demonstrated on psychomotor development (Mora *et al.*, 1974), sensorimotor intelligence (Christiansen *et al.*, 1974: Dasen, Inhelder *et al.*, 1978), general levels of activity, and some aspects of infant—mother interactions (Klein *et al.*, 1974). However, the relationships are not very strong, and rather unsystematic. A general conclusion is that socioeconomic and sociocultural variables are usually more important than moderate malnutrition. It is still unclear as to whether the efects of moderate malnutrition are permanent.

Most of the studies on the developmental effects of malnutrition have been carried out in South and Central America. Among those which took place in Africa is an early study by Stock and Smythe (1967) in which twenty children who had been severely malnourished during infancy were followed up for eleven years, and their performance on a series of psychological tests was compared to a "control group" of children of the same sex and age who had not suffered from malnutrition. The undernourished children performed significantly less well than the control group on a general intelligence test. Particularly on sub-tests measuring visual-motor ability, and pattern perception (spatial skills) they showed a poorer grasp of the concept of time, lower motivation on an achievement-oriented task, less initiative, a lower level of organization of play material, some indications of lower school achievement, and a larger proportion of abnormal EEG records. The author attributed these differences to organic brain damage, but the results are not really convincing, because "although both groups were drawn from the lowest socioeconomic level, the disparity of their living conditions was very marked. Alcoholism, illegitimacy and broken homes were the rule in the undernourished group, whereas the control groups lived under more stable home conditions". Such a confusion with a sociocultural difference is very typical of this sort of study.

A much more careful matching of previously malnourished children with a control group was done in a study in Uganda (Hoorweg, 1976), with very similar results: "There is a general impairment of intellectual abilities (in previously severely and chronically malnourished children), with reasoning and spatial abilities most affected, memory and rote learning intermediately affected, and language ability least, if at all, affected".

The effects of moderate malnutrition were studied by Sieye (1975) in urban and peri-urban children in Abidjan. No statistically significant relationship was found between nutritional status, psychomotor development, and sensorimotor intelligence in the first two years of life, and malnutrition at age 2 was not related to psychological-test performance at age 4. The mal-nourished children were more often passive during the examinations, and there are some indications that they performed better than well nourished children on some items of the Casati and Lézine (1968) scale at 12 months, whereas they performed less well at 15–18 months. Sieye hypothesizes that the onset of malnutrition may initially have an activating effect through compensatory mechanisms such as the stimulation of growth hormone, the negative effect appearing after some time if the malnutrition persists.

Also in the Ivory Coast, in a rural sample, Dasen, Lavallée et al. (1977) (and see Dasen, Inhelder et al., 1978) found a small effect of moderate malnutrition on the development of sensorimotor intelligence. The dif-ference between the two groups was statistically significant on half of the items of the Casati and Lézine (1968) scale, and although the effect occurs throughout the age-range tested (6 to 31 months), it is particularly notice-able during the stage of "active experimentation" on the environment. While the development of well-nourished children was quite systematically advanced over French norms, the malnourished children showed an advance on one subscale only. The "activating effect" hypothesized by Sieye (1975) was not found. A trend also occurs indicating a negative effect of moderate malnutrition on the development of the "semiotic function", the symbolic activities which follow the stage of sensorimotor intelligence. While the effects of moderate malnutrition on psychological development are not very systematic, these results call for programmes designed to improve the health and nutritional environment of African children.

Having examined the psychomotor and affective aspects of development during infancy, we shall consider in the next chapter another important aspect — intellectual development.

7

CHILD DEVELOPMENT
(2) INTELLECTUAL DEVELOPMENT

PSYCHOLOGISTS have many ways of looking at cognitive development, and many ways to define intelligence. Basic cognitive mechanisms, such as visual perception or memory, can be included under this heading. Many interesting studies have been carried out in Africa, aptly summarized and discussed by Dague (1970a and b), Lloyd (1972), Serpell (1976), Wober (1975) and others. The general conclusion which emerges is that basic intellectual mechanisms are universal, but that environment determines the situations in which they are applied (Cole and Scribner, 1974). Similarly, basic perceptual mechanisms are universal, but different visual ecologies lead to different interpretations of the same visual cues (Segal *et al.*, 1966).

The influence of the environment cannot be discounted in any aspect of psychological functioning, but it is beyond the scope of this report to provide an exhaustive coverage of the field. Rather, we prefer to select one approach which has already led to the accumulation of an extensive body of data and which seems promising for future research and application, and deal with this topic in some detail. We have chosen the theory of Jean Piaget, for the following reasons: it is an interactionist position, taking into account both biological factors such as maturation and environmental influences; there are strong indications that the theory has some universal validity; it has far-reaching implications for educational applications.

This choice does not mean that other avenues of psychological research on intellectual development are fruitless. There is excellent work, for example, in the American tradition of concept formation research, or in recent approaches to psychometric tests and factor analysis (Wober, 1975).

On the other hand, one avenue which does seem to have led to a dead end is the tradition of intelligence testing, including the search for so-called "culture-free" or "culture-fair" tests. In the early history of this movement, it was believed that intelligence tests could measure some sort of innate capacity while the influence of the environment was neglected completely. These early studies used instruments that were developed and calibrated in Western societies to test African children. The fallacy of this approach has been pointed out repeatedly (e.g. Jahoda *et al.*, 1974; Biesheuvel, 1959). In attempting to devise "culture-free" tests, psychologists were trying to eliminate the environment instead of studying its effects; but this attempt failed. Finally it has been suggested that intelligence must be defined differently in different environments. Vernon (1969) writes:

> We must try to discard the idea that intelligence is a kind of universal faculty, a trait which is the same (apart from variations in amount) in all cultural groups. Clearly it develops differently in different physical and cultural environments. (p. 10).

Berry (1974) proposes a position of radical cultural relativism with respect to the concept of intelligence. Intelligence can be better described by those various cognitive skills which are developed in, and valued by a particular cultural group.

Some, but not many studies have been carried out on how particular cultural groups define "intelligence". Wober (1975) found that the Kiganda of Uganda saw intelligence more as "wisdom", incorporating social skills but bearing no relationship to the Western idea of speed in performance. In West Africa, Bisilliat *et al.* (1967) studied the notion of "lakkal" in the Djerma-Songhai culture, and found that it could not be completely translated by "intelligence" because it includes knowledge, curiosity, learning skills, social integration and, generally speaking, the capability to integrate in one's own environment. We may give some thought to the possibility that such a definition of "intelligence" may be more in keeping with maintaining a balanced ecology than the Western definition, which is associated with individuality and competition.

As we now turn to a survey of research on Piagetian concept development in Africa, we may want to keep in mind that Piaget, too, has defined intelligence as adaptation to the environment, even though he may have developed his theory from the point of view of his own culture, which values highly technological and scientific concepts.

PURPOSES OF PIAGETIAN RESEARCH IN AFRICA

Most of the early studies, and some of the more recent ones, have replicated Piaget's work, for the purpose of testing the generality of his concepts across different cultures. Investigators have been particularly interested to test in different populations Piaget's proposal that children's thought develops through a definite sequence of stages, each of which has its own unique characteristics. Possible differences in performance between ethnic groups as well as among sub-groups of various cultures have also been explored. Increasing numbers of studies have been designed to investigate other variables which may be responsible for differences in performance.

In Western, technological environments, it has been found with only a very few exceptions, that all children do follow the same sequence of developmental levels. There are many different areas of cognitive or conceptual development in Piaget's theory (e.g. elementary logic, number, measurement, conservation, space, speed, time, mental imagery, memory) and although it has been assumed, on theoretical grounds, that the progression in one area should be congruent with the progression in all other areas, the correspondence is in fact less than perfect.

Piaget has described the following sequence of major states:

(1) *Sensorimotor intelligence*: the development of a basic understanding of the world in the first two years of life; there are definite reasoning processes even at this early age, expressed in action rather than language.

(2) *The pre-operational stage*: the child learns to use symbols, particularly language, but his reasoning is usually limited to taking only one aspect of a situation into account. This formative stage has often been defined by what the child cannot do which he can do later, but research is now under way to describe the reasoning processes at this stage in more positive terms.

(3) *The concrete operational stage*: the child can now take two or several aspects of a situation into account, and can coordinate them according to simple logical laws; the reasoning is very much dependent on the content which is why this stage does not appear all at once, but at different ages depending on the difficulty of each particular concept.

(4) *The formal operational stage*: the reasoning is no longer bound to real situations but can be applied to pure hypotheses, which can be tested through systematic verification. Formal reasoning, in its fullest development, is the reasoning of the scientist.

The reasoning at each stage can be defined in terms of particular logical structures, but we shall not go into the details of Piaget's formulations.

It is generally agreed that the sequence of stages (and of the sub-stages within each stage for each particular concept) is identical in all humans, in other words that it is universal. On the other hand, the ages at which the different levels are attained may change under the influence of the environment. This general conclusion is of course an oversimplification, and we must consider each of Piaget's main developmental stages in some detail.

The sensorimotor stage

It is only very gradually that the simple reflexes of the newborn baby become complex actions, through which the baby can explore his world and thus get to understand it. For example, if an object is hidden in front of a young baby's eyes, he first reacts as if the object had disappeared, as if it did not exist any more. At a later stage, the baby will be able to reach for the hidden object, but if the object is then placed under a second cover, he will search at the first location even though he has seen the object being hidden elsewhere. Such observations have led Piaget to believe that objects, for the very young infant, are not permanent, in other words that "object permanence" is not innate but has to be learned. Similarly, the baby gradually learns to solve problems such as retrieving an object which is out of reach with the help of an instrument such as a stick, or by pulling on the cloth which supports the object. There are many such observations which indicate the infant's increasing understanding of his environment, and of the effects of his actions on it.

No cross-cultural study had been done in this area, probably because of the lack of standardized observation techniques. However there are now several ordinal scales based on Piaget's early observations (Casati and Lézine, 1968; Lézine, Stambak and Casati, 1969; Kopp and Sigman, 1972; Kopp, Sigman and Parmelee, 1974; Uzgiris and Hunt, 1975; Corman and Escalona, 1969) and these have been expertly characterized and discussed by Uzgiris (1976).

The development of sensorimotor intelligence in African infants has been studied by Dasen, Inhelder *et al.* (1978) in a sample of rural Baoule children in the Ivory Coast, using the Casati and Lézine (1968) scale. A statistically significant advance on French norms was found on three sub-scales (the use of an instrument to retrieve an object and two problems involving the combination of objects) throughout all relevant stages and the whole age range (from 5 to 31 months). On other sub-scales, there usually was some advance on French norms, but it was not statistically significant at all stages. This finding confirms Super's notion of a limited African precocity, and extends it from motor to intellectual development. However Dasen and his colleagues' study was not designed to link the findings to specific infant-training practices or cultural values. In fact, the greatest precocity occurs in sub-scales which involve the handling of objects, and this may come as a surprise in view of the majority of the literature which has tended to describe the African infant as passive in an environment which is poor in objects (Richards, 1932; Ashton, 1952; Knappen, 1962; Erny, 1972a); furthermore, African cultural values stress social interactions rather than object manipulation (Zempléni-Rabain, 1970; Valantin, 1970, 1972).

Mundy-Castle and Okonji (1976) report a similar observation among rural Igbo carried out by Whiten and Whiten. Opportunities for early object manipulation were similar for English and Igbo children. "However, later interactions of mother and baby with objects revealed what may be an important difference. In Oxford, a lot of mother-infant interaction is focused on objects, whereas in (Nigeria) none of this type of interaction was seen, apart from the mother giving an object to play with. Mothers did not seem to play object-games with their children." Thus, Euro-American babies would have greater experience of handling objects, and their attention would be "more often focused on objective properties of reality" whereas "African babies receive more social stimulation and early emotional support . . . The issue here is whether in the long run this divergent stimulation brings about a differential patterning of cognitive development, with Africans acquiring an intelligence that is more socially oriented, Europeans one that is more technologically oriented" (Mundy-Castle, 1976).

Dasen, Inhelder et al. (1978) agree with the common statement that the African rural environment is usually poor in toys and other structured, technological objects and that mother-child interactions are usually not focused on objects. However, in their naturalistic behaviour observations, they found the babies manipulating objects, exploring them, combining them, then using them in meaningful seqeunces, either conventionally (i.e. each object in its usual function) or symbolically (i.e. using an object to represent something else) in much the same way and at about the same ages as Western children, although no quantitative comparison is offered to support the latter claim. They remark that the environment is rich in unstructured objects (sticks, stones, cooking implements, tins, etc.) which are particularly favourable for symbolic use, and the child is absolutely free to explore all objects, including dangerous ones.

These observations do not support the passivity said to characterize African children. In this respect, Dasen, Inhelder et al. (1978) do not deny that African children, especially older ones, can often remain quiet (passive) for long periods, particularly in the presence of adults or a foreign observer: this manifest control seems to be required as a sign of respect to elders. Furthermore, in a structured situation where the infants were presented with a fixed array of objects, Dasen and his colleagues describe a more quiet style in the handling of objects than is usual in Western children, and in some cases a more restricted use of space, but they claim that the structure of the activities observed is identical in Baoule and Western children.

Beyond the stages of simple object manipulation, they also observed the symbolic use of objects. The latter is, of course, derived from the imitation of familiar models, thus a young Baoule child is likely to imitate the activities of carrying water on the head or pounding yams in a mortar, whereas a French child is more likely to sit his doll on the chamber pot. The content of these symbolic activities is different and related to cultural models, but they indicate the same level of cognitive development.

The finding of an identical succession of stages in sensorimotor intelligence, with a precocity in the rate of development in some areas, has been supported independently by Sieye (1975) in a study of urban and peri-urban infants in Abidjan (Ivory Coast). Goldberg (1972), on the other hand, in a study using the Corman and Escalona (1969) scale in Lusaka (Zambia), reports a slight advance on American norms at 6 months and a slight lag at 9 and 12 months. But she mentions difficulties in establishing rapport because of a very strong reaction to strangers, and similarly in Bovet and his collaborators' (1974) study in the Ivory Coast, the decline in the second year could have been due to such problems. Both Sieye (1975) and Dasen, Inhelder et al. (1978) insist on the importance of establishing a congenial testing atmosphere in such studies, especially in view of the fact that the situations in the sensorimotor scales are often frustrating, for example when an object is hidden or when it is placed out of immediate reach. The latter authors remark that very often, the initial reaction of the Baoule infant is to cry, expecting the mother to react immediately in reaching the object for him (or to let him suck the breast instead). The experimenter then has to rule out this initial way of solving the problem while still maintaining the child's motivation; it is only if he manages to do this that the infant is able to solve the problem through other, more cognitive, means.

The detailed study of infant behaviour has made enormous progress with the advent, over the past 15 years, of experimental laboratory studies (e.g. Stone, Smith and Murphy, 1974; Bower, 1974a and b); since these usually require very sophisticated apparatus, no cross-cultural replications have been carried out in Africa, with the exception of an ongoing project in Lagos on visual search and scanning strategies in very young babies. Mundy-Castle (1978) reports the emergence of the same patterns of looking at much the same ages in Nigerian and American babies.

In conclusion, cognitive (intellectual) development during infancy follows the same pattern in Africa as in European or American children and most likely, as in children all over the world. The basic mechanisms of human cognition are truly universal. However, even at this early age, development is not independent of its cultural context. The impact of the environment, for example through different value systems and child-rearing practices, can be seen to some extent in the different behaviour style and content, and in some differences in the rates of development.

The concrete operational stage

This second stage, and its formative period, called the pre-operational period, is of direct relevance to the nursery and primary school teacher, and it is on this stage that most cross-cultural research has been carried out. It is generally concluded from cross-sectional studies (although longitudinal ones would be more to the point), that those children who attain the last sub-stage of this period all reach it after having followed the same sequence, for each particular concept. Some children, however, do not seem to reach the last sub-stage in some conceptual areas. Whether this is true only at the performance level (the answers given to particular tasks in particular experimental situations) or also at the competence level (the actual capacity of reasoning) is one of the controversial areas being investigated currently.

Conservation concepts

Many studies have dealt with one aspect of the concrete operational stage which deals with the construction of "invariance", the idea that some physical properties of an object are not changed (i.e. remain invariant or are "conserved") even when the perceptual aspects are transformed. For example, the "conservation of number" refers to the fact that ten objects remain ten whether they are placed in a line or in a circle, a property of number which is not obvious to the young child. Similarly, if one of two identical balls of clay is rolled out, or flattened, neither its "quantity" nor its weight nor its volume change, but this is only understood gradually by children between the ages of about 5 to 12 years. Many similar situations have been devised by Piaget, relating to the conservation not only of quantity, weight, volume and number but also length, area, etc.

The studies carried out on such conservation concepts in Africa are summarized in Table 1 in Appendix 3. The following conclusions emerge:

Intercultural comparisons Many of the studies have included comparative studies across or within cultures. Direct intercultural comparisons have been made by Beard (1968), Poole (1968), Heron and Simonsson (1969), Vernon (1969), Hendrikz (1966) and Goldschmid *et al.* (1973). All showed that African children were behind Europeans in their performance on the operational task, but in no case were efforts made to check on the subjects' understanding of the problem.

Indirect comparisons, that is comparisons with results obtained in other studies, have been made by Price-Williams (1961), Lloyd (1971a and b), Ohuche (1971), Kamara and Easley (1977) and Nyiti (1977), who found little or no difference between African and European performance.

Indirect comparisons, however, have limited value in this respect, since results of different researchers sometimes show considerable variation of performance on the same task. Particular attention, however, should be given to the work of Kamara and Easley (1977) and Nyiti (1977), who both reduced intercultural differences by using refined methods of determining age, and by taking precautions within a flexible interview technique to ensure that the subject understood the problem in a relevant cultural context and had adequate opportunity to display his competence.

The results suggest that intercultural differences are least when the research involves:

(a) Subjects from the elite classes;
(b) Simpler tasks;
(c) A flexible clinical method, rather than standardized interviews;
(d) An accomplished interviewer from the same culture as the third-world sample; and
(e) Adequate training procedures.

Intracultural comparisons Intracultural comparisons have employed several different dimensions. For instance, Etuk (1967) and Lloyd (1971a and b) both found that children from "modern homes" were superior in performance to those from "traditional" backgrounds. Both used the mother's education as the criterion for determining the modern/traditional classification.

The urban/rural dimension has been employed by Greenfield (1966), Poole (1968), Kirk (1977), and Owoc (1973). No consistent results emerge from these studies, but only Kirk described her sample in any detail. She found that, over all, elite children performed better than village children, who in turn performed better than those from crowded urban areas.

Schooling has provided some advantage to children in the studies of Greenfield (1966), Kamara and Easley (1977), Okonji (1971a) and Owoc (1973), and this difference often increases with age. Several of these researchers, using older subjects, have reported evidence that in the absence of schooling, a substantial proportion of the population may never succeed on the tasks used.

Kiminyo (1977) and Nyiti (1977), on the other hand, found no differences between their schooled and unschooled samples. It may be, as in intercultural comparisons, that able testers, suffering no linguistic or cultural handicaps, are able to elicit better performance from unschooled children, who otherwise may respond more slowly and in unexpected ways when compared to their schooled counterparts.

Several studies have attempted to correlate environmental variables with performance on Piagetian tasks. Vernon (1969) in Uganda found that economic status and cultural stimulus had significant loadings in a factor analysis. Kirk (1977) and Adjei (1977), both working in Ghana, found that some aspects of maternal behaviour in a teaching situation correlated with the child's performance on Piagetian tasks, although Adjei's correlations were weak and inconsistent. Adjei also found that both children and adults with pottery-making experience tended to perform better on conservation tasks than subjects without that experience.

Classification tasks

A second type of task from the period of concrete operations which has been widely used in Africa is classification. Inhelder and Piaget (1964) used a variety of classification tasks to investigate the development of structures of mental operations in children. Most later studies in Africa, unlike those in which conservation tasks were used, were not conducted for the purpose of investigating any aspect of Piaget's theory, but mainly to assess children's abilities to abstract as judged by such criteria as flexibility in shifting bases of classification, use of superordinate concepts, and type of basis (colour form, function, etc.) preferred for classification. These classification tasks, by themselves, have limited use in diagnosing the developmental stage achieved, according to Inhelder and Piaget (1964), since the concrete operational structure of classification is attained only when class-inclusion is also mastered. Hendrikz (1966), Etuk (1967), Otaala (1971a), Tapé (1977) and Lavallée and Dasen (1979) have included a test of this ability. A summary of the studies of classification, is given in Table 2 of Appendix 3.

Drawing general conclusions from these studies is made difficult by the differences in methodology, the variety of purpose for which the studies were undertaken, and the variation in performance resulting from the use of different materials. Only two conclusions can be stated with reasonable conviction:
(a) Performance depends to a great extent on familiarity with the material to be classified and the bases of classification;
(b) The use of abstraction increases with increasing age.
In studies where constraints have been imposed, colour seems to have been preferred to other attributes as the basis for sorting, but this finding may not be generally valid since these cases usually involve test materials with which the subjects were unfamiliar. In the case of Gay and his collaborators (Gay and Cole, 1967; Cole *et al.*, 1971), the discovery of the problems which Kpelle persons encountered with classifying unfamiliar objects led to the investigation of culturally relevant methods of classification. A similarly fruitful line of investigation was adopted by Fjellman (1969) who, after dis-

cussions with adults, selected wild animals as a semantic domain with which rural Akamba children of Kenya were familiar, and developed appropriate tests to examine the formal characteristics of the children's sorting. In both cases, colour was not used as an important criterion in the children's classification, and children were able to form classes on the basis of more abstract characteristics.

Space concepts

Another important aspect of concept development is the understanding of the location of objects (or places) and their interrelationships. According to Piaget (1948), the young child starts to understand *topological* spatial relationships first: these are simple concepts such as next to, on, curved vs. straight, open vs. closed, etc. Later, the child acquires *projective* concepts (directions, angles, point of view) and *Euclidean* concepts (distances, spatial coordinates). These concepts are needed to understand geometry and geography at school and, in daily life, for spatial orientation beyond the immediate neighbourhood.

Kidd and Rivoire (1965) analysed the spatial items of so-called "culture-free" tests, and found that topological properties seemed to be universal whereas cultural differences are found in the development of projective and Euclidean concepts. Piagetian tasks of space concepts were used in studies in various parts of Africa by de Lemos (1974), Beard (1968), Vernon (1969), Page (1973), Jahoda, Deregowski and Sinha (1974), Omari (1975, 1977), Dasen (1975, 1977a) and Kirk (1977). The following findings emerge:
(a) Piaget's sequence of stages is confirmed in the main lines;
(b) Intercultural differences are least in tasks involving topological concepts;
(c) Projective and Euclidean relationships emerge relatively late and several studies report that many African children have not completely mastered these concepts by the end of primary school.
In this respect, the results of studies on spatial concepts seem to differ from those on conservation and classification concepts: all schooled children acquire the conservation of quantity and weight concepts and classification concepts by age 12–14 years at the latest, whereas this is not the case for the more difficult space concepts. That spatial skills seem to present a special problem is also supported by studies with psychometric tests (e.g. Berry, 1976) and by observations in the practice of teaching science and technology (e.g. Deregowski, 1971).

Berry (1976) has suggested that spatial skills are not as highly valued in sedentary, agricultural societies as in nomadic, hunting societies where these skills are needed for survival. Dasen (1975, 1977a) has applied this ecocultural model to Piagetian concept development, showing that in two samples of nomadic, hunting people (Eskimos and Australian Aborigines), space concepts developed rapidly whereas conservation concepts developed only very slowly, whereas in a sample of a sedentary, agricultural group (in Ivory Coast) the reverse was true. Dasen hypothesized that conservation concepts would be more highly valued if food is grown, stored and exchanged on markets.

This differential development of concrete operational concepts, depending on ecocultural demands, implies a strong environmental influence on concept development. It also implies that it is not possible to assign any individual (and even less a group) to a single cognitive level or "developmental status" (Cole and Scribner, 1977). Depending on which conceptual area is studied, and which task is used, the resulting inference as to the level of development would be quite different. The ecocultural framework also implies that no value judgment should be attached to different rates of development (Dasen, Berry and Witkin, 1979).

Training studies

A number of the studies reviewed have shown that intercultural differences are reduced if children are compared who live in an urban environment, and come from higher socioeconomic strata, in other words are brought up in a more Westernized, technological environment. Is it possible to reduce intercultural differences through direct, short-term intervention, without changing anything in the environment and culture? Several training studies have been carried out to answer this question (Dasen, Lavallée and Retschitzki, 1979; Lavallée and Dasen, 1979; Dasen, Lavallée and Ngini, 1979). These authors used training techniques for Piagetian concepts in the three areas reviewed above (Conservation of Quantity, Quantification of Class Inclusion, and Spatial Coordinates) with children from both West and East Africa. The authors conclude that, in the case of their studies at least, intercultural differences could be greatly reduced or completely bridged by adequate training techniques.

These training studies are also relevant to the competence/performance distinction: are there real intercultural or inter-group differences in the attainment of operational structures, or only in the performance of tests? Dasen and his associates tentatively conclude from their studies that differences occur both in competence and performance, depending on the concept studied and the age of the children.

The stage of formal operations

This is the third and last stage in Piaget's sequence, and is of special interest to the secondary-school teacher: in particular, the successful achievement of secondary-school mathematics, physics and chemistry seem to depend on the reasoning processes of this stage. In Western countries, the assumption that all adults are able to use formal operations seems to be questioned by recent evidence (Modgil and Modgil, 1976). In any case, it seems that adults reason formally only in some instances, and often not on Piaget's tasks, which are strongly oriented towards physics, chemistry and mathematics.

As part of an extensive study in Rwanda, Laurendeau (1977) used a task of formal operations involving the comparison of proportions (Quantification of Probabilities). In a group of 15–17 year old pupils with normal schooling, the majority gave answers typical of the first sub-stages of formal operations and only a small proportion (ten to twenty-five per cent) seemed to have reached the last sub-stage. In other groups with limited schooling (3 or 6 years) or no schooling at all, all subjects gave concrete operational answers.

Eunice Okeke (1976) evaluated the level of understanding of three biological concepts by Nigerian candidates in the West African School Certificate Examination. She interviewed a sample of 120 pupils from eight schools on their understanding of each concept. By relating the answers to the developmental psychology of Piaget, it was possible to determine the frequency with which the subjects applied formal reasoning. It was discovered that most of the pupils applied concrete operational reasoning even on those questions requiring formal thought.

Pearson carried out an extensive research programme in Ghana, adapting several concrete and formal operational tasks for group administration in preparation for an extensive, nationwide survey of reasoning abilities in secondary school pupils. The formal operational tasks used were the combination of chemicals, quantification of probabilities, and curves of movement, all of which gave equivalent results in the individual and group forms, and for different experimenters. Pupils in forms 1 and 3 were consistently at the last sub-stage on conservation of quantity (liquids) and weight, but not on the conservation of volume, and only a small proportion gave a consistent formal operational performance.

The studies on formal operational reasoning are too few to reach any firm conclusions, and the impact of environmental factors has not yet been studied with the exception of schooling in Laurendeau's research. Piaget and Inhelder's original tasks are clearly relevant in a secondary-school situation, but hardly outside this very restricted segment of the population. It has sometimes been suggested that one should do away with all tasks and testing situations, and study Piagetian concepts in real-life situations, but unfortunately this is more easily said than done.

SOME METHODOLOGICAL PROBLEMS

In considering the tentative conclusions which we have drawn from this body of research, it is wise to refer to some precedural problems that have been associated with many of these studies; even if some of these may appear somewhat technical, a note of caution is necessary to avoid unwarranted generalizations. Information relevant to the first five of the problems listed below appears in Table 1 of Appendix 3; points (a), (b) and (g) have been discussed in detail by Kamara and Easley (1977).

(a) Language presents a problem where the local language is not the medium of instruction. A choice has to be made as to whether children should be tested in the vernacular, or in the language in which they are undergoing formal education. The latter will often be less familiar to the children, particularly the younger ones, but it will be more convenient for the non-indigenous tester.

The translation of questions and instructions from one language to another presents great difficulties in establishing functional equivalence. Vernon (1969) tested entirely in English. Heron and Simonsson (1969) avoided the problem by using a non-verbal method. The effect of language on performance is not known, although Margaret Earle found that twelve-year-old Ghanaian boys performed equally well in both vernacular and English on Vernon's (1965) battery of tests.

(b) The use of a tester from another culture raises problems, some of which are also connected with language. Unfavourable interactions between subjects and testers have been found in societies where interracial tensions exist, but no conclusions can be drawn from these studies which would be valid for work in most parts of Africa.* In many studies, foreign researchers have trained members of the target culture to administer the tests.

(c) While most studies have used individual testing, two have made use of paper and pencil tests administered to groups (Beard, 1968; Poole, 1968). The effect on performance of this variation is not known, except in Pearson's study where performance on individual and group tests were equivalent for some tasks but not for others.

(d) Too little overlap in choice of tasks presents yet another problem for comparison. About eight different conservation tasks have been used, but over half of the studies employed no more than two at a time, and few of these used any other type of Piagetian task.

This presents problems of interpretation, since success on tasks presumably related to the same cognitive structures are not achieved at the same time, and may be attained in different orders in different cultures.

(e) Problems due to lack of standardized procedures for administering tasks appear in a number of ways. In some studies the procedure, or materials used have been modified to such an extent from the original tasks used by Piaget's workers, as to raise the possibility that the very nature of the task itself has been altered. In many others, slighter modifications, the effects of which are known, have been made. Performance may be enhanced by use of familiar materials, but this proposition has not yet been tested adequately. It is known that in Western societies, performance on various Piagetian tasks may be affected by the nature of the task, even though identical basic problems are involved (Lovell and Slater, 1960; Szeminska, 1965), by the use of different materials (Uzgiris, 1964; Szeminska, 1965; Guyler, 1969), and by the type of response required (Pratoomraj and Johnson, 1966). On the other hand, some workers in non-Western societies have specifically stated that performance was unaffected by the materials used (de Lemos, 1969; Roll, 1970; Lloyd, 1971b). (In the fifth column of Table 1 in Appendix 3, a "Yes" indicates what we consider to be a significant modification of the task or of materials used.)

* However, in Pearson's study in Ghana, the race or sex of the tester had no systematic effect.

(f) Great ranges in the criteria by which successful performance is judged can also be found. Many researchers have not required explanations for the children's answers, and those that have exhibited great variation in the degree of consistency that they required.

(g) The determination of the age of the subjects has presented serious problems to many researchers who have for the most part resorted to rough estimates or have accepted the subjects' own statements of age. Kamara's work (1971; Kamara and Easley, 1977) suggests that one way to solve this problem is to make use of indigenous methods of telling age. Kirk (1975, 1977) has developed a method based on dental eruption.

SUMMARY OF ENVIRONMENTAL INFLUENCES

Conceptual development occurs through the interaction of the organism's biological background (brain structure and maturation) with the environment. This interaction occurs at such a general level, that it produces in every individual the same basic cognitive structures, which develop through an identical sequence of stages. Beyond this basic "unity of mankind", however, different environments also produce differences in behaviour, not in the basic mechanisms themselves but in the way they are applied in particular situations. Basically, human behaviour is adaptive: people develop those skills and concepts which they need (Berry, 1974), through the mediation of culture (which includes child rearing and socialization practices, language, values and social structure) and in relation to ecological demands. Thus different cultures value different intellectual skills.

But the environment is changing; in some parts of Africa, under the influence of industrialization and urbanization, it is changing very rapidly. Much more research is needed to specify how these changes affect intellectual development, but keeping in mind the limitations outlined above, we may tentatively conclude that such environmental variables as urbanization, social class and educational services do affect intellectual development. These variables, however, are "packaged" (Whiting, 1976). They have not been refined enough; much more research is needed to break them down into components, and to determine which one, or which combination has an effect on cognitive development. In other words, in addition to demonstrating an environmental effect, its specific mechanism has to be elucidated.

8
PROSPECTS, OBSERVATIONS AND RECOMMENDATIONS

INTRODUCTION

Up to this point we have discussed the existing conditions affecting the child in Africa as he interacts with his environment. Aspects of this discussion have been the empirical studies presented primarily in Chapters 6 and 7. Other parts of the discussion have been in the form of a review of services available to the child as he grows and develops. The object of this chapter is to make observations and recommendations expected to be useful to those already involved or to those who might wish to become involved in projects, programmes and enterprises to aid the child in this part of the world and to enable him to derive maximum benefits from what is hoped will be his ever-improving environment. At the top of this list are the African governments, institutions, and people.

OBSERVATIONS

We shall begin by noting the progress which the various African countries have made in providing appropriate services to children, since the attainment of their independence. Of particular note is the important role which all of these countries have defined for the education of youth. Properly conceived, education should enable an individual to understand his environment, gain a measure of control over it and, at the appropriate time, make positive contributions towards its improvement. It is therefore with joy that we note that, in all African countries, education is now viewed as an important instrument of national development. Not only is the amount of education being provided increasing, but, what is even more encouraging, in the last few years positive steps have been taken towards making schools more relevant to the communities in which they exist. Except for inherited colonial institutions and methods, which were established without due regard to the environments in which they were created, education is now expected to help bring about a new world economic order of the type African countries desire and deserve.

Also encouraging is the fact that education is no longer narrowly limited to the confines of school education. As indicated in the *Final Report* of the Lagos Conference of Ministers of Education (UNESCO, 1976: p. 14):

> The vast majority of African countries have already attacked the problem of supplementing and articulating school education with various types of adult and out-of-school education . . .
> Youth training schemes and national civic services for participation in national development have been created. Provision has been made for school leavers who cannot continue their studies and are not in a position to find productive employment. In many cases the school becomes a community centre which caters for the needs of both children and adults.

These efforts are both commendable and remarkable. We also commend the efforts of all the African countries to provide institutions for children who need special care, and the efforts of some countries in encouraging agencies developing facilities for the care of children of working mothers. Moreover, in a few countries major breakthroughs are being made with programmes directed towards integrated rural development. The major strides that have been made in various countries in the direction of providing antenatal, postnatal, and school clinics and other medical facilities that benefit children is noted and appreciated.

Finally, the enthusiasm with which African countries have embraced the concept of the International Year of the Child (IYC) should be recognized. In various African countries, national committees have been created and are busy planning activities. Some countries have gone one step further, adding state or provincial committees to the national ones. Others have gone further still by adding local government committees in an attempt to ensure that the concept gets grass roots support and participation. The three authors who visited some African countries in connection with this project note with pride and satisfaction the ready help provided to us by government functionaries and other citizens with whom we held discussions. It is also pleasing to note that in many countries major research projects connected with child development are taking place at the moment.

In Mauritius, with the approval of the Ministry of Health, and under the sponsorship of the Ministry of Education, a programme entitled the Joint Health and Education Project was established some time ago. The joint Health and Education Project in Mauritius is part of a larger international project researching the possibility of identifying mental illness at an early age, before the emergence of patterns of behaviour which are difficult to change. The project also enquires as to the feasibility of intervening in the development of children who risk later mental illness.

In order to achieve a reasonable level of success on such a programme, the help of paramedical and medical personnel has been secured through the Ministry of Health. This programme not only integrates children and parents, but also the services available in the region where the units are functioning.

In Nigeria, a major study has been undertaken connected with the rehabilitation of children displaced during the Nigerian Civil war. It is one of many studies now taking place in the departments of sociology, education and psychology at several different universities. Another major investigation is the Six Year Project, at Ife University, which deals with mother-tongue education.

Since its inception more than fifteen years ago, the Human Development Research Unit (HDRU), at the University of Zambia, has encouraged studies on many aspects of child development. A number of studies with topics such as psychomotor development, perception and cognitive development have been conducted. Recent studies have included the study of short-term memory in children, stress in adolescents, and achievement motivation in secondary-school children.

In Kenya, research work on children was begun on a large scale when the Child Development Research Unit (now the Bureau of Educational Research) was established about ten years ago. So far, studies covering aspects of the child's development, such as psychomotor development and socialization, have been carried out.

A recent project at the Bureau of Educational Research was the investigation of the relationship of family background variables, socialization practices, and daily activities to cognitive development and school performance. The study took advantage of a massive amount of data on one single community collected over the years. In this data, extensive mother-child interactions were observed and could be related to the cognitive performance of the same children years later. The cognitive measures in this study comprise an array of Piagetian concepts in the areas of space, conservation and classification, non-verbal psychometric tests of spatial skills and memory, and psychological differentiation.*

An extensive research project on the ecological correlates and determinants of psychological differentiation is taking place in the Central African Republic. It compares various aspects of cognitive style and socialization practices in agricultural Bantu and hunting Pygmy populations (Berry, Witkin and associates). Extensive research on cognitive style is also under way at the National University of Zaire, under the direction of Nkanga Kalemba-Vita, who is also studying other aspects of cognitive development, such as creativity and logical reasoning.

Also in Zaire, the African Bureau of Education (B.A.S.E.) in Kisangani is carrying out a number of research projects dealing with child development and education. Examples include a study of the difficulties pupils encounter when they first enter primary school, a critical analysis of mathematics textbooks used in primary schools in Zaire, and the role of education in national and, in particular, in rural development.

In Upper-Volta, several psychological studies related to pre-school and primary school education are under way at the Institut National d'Education (I.N.E.). One study is of school-failure in the present system, which should help in the restructuring of the whole educational system.

In Bamako, Mali, research on cognitive development, mainly along the lines of Piaget's theory, is in progress at the Ecole Normale Supérieure under the direction of Professor Mohamud Cisse. Studies have already been carried out by teacher-trainees on the acquisition of concrete and formal operations

---

* The theory of psychological differentiation has been developed over the years by Witkin and associates (Witkin, 1962). It began with the discovery that some individuals were more capable than others of using their own body information in judging the gravitational vertical, and in picking out a small figure from a complex design. These individuals were termed "field-independent", because they seemed to be less dependent on, or less influenced by, the visual environment than others. Field-independent people also seemed to be more individualistic in social interactions, less influenced by public opinion, but also less sensitive to social situations and less sociable. Psychological differentiation is influenced by socialization practices; children whose mothers encourage self-reliance, autonomy, internal control of impulses, and use lenient discipline, tend to be more field-independent. The cross-cultural extension of this theory has been reviewed by Witkin and Berry (1975) and Okonji (in press). In particular, it seems that different ecocultural settings foster psychological differentiation; in nomadic hunting and gathering societies, field-independence and its correlates are valued, in sedentary, agricultural societies, field-dependence and its associated social skills seem to be more adaptive (Berry, 1976).

in various sub-groups of children and adolescents. Similarly, at the Ecole Normale Supérieure in Abidjan, Ivory Coast, interesting research on child development is being carried out by Professor Gozé Tapé (1977; Kihm and Tapé, 1977) and at the newly formed Department of Psychology, at the University of Abidjan, by Professor Kouadio Aka.

Many other studies in other parts of Africa could be mentioned. Some deal with the structure and sequencing of curricula; others deal with attitudes of young learners, others are directed towards teacher effectiveness. What has been mentioned in this section is a small random sample, supplementing the studies indicated in earlier chapters of this book. That all of these investigations involving children, directly or indirectly, are taking place is clearly a sign of positive development, related to the over-all improvement of the environment of the child in Africa.

Nevertheless, it is our opinion that certain basic ingredients are lacking, and their absence tends to make the progress achieved in education, public health, and medical care seem insignificant. Perhaps the simplest way to indicate the missing link is to state that in many African countries planning appears haphazard, unrealistic, unimaginative and for the most part unrelated to the environment. For instance, many countries spend about twenty per cent of their annual budget to maintain a formal school system which benefits less than fifty per cent of the school-age population and do next to nothing for the majority of the children who are outside the formal school structure. Only a fundamental change in structure and strategy, based upon proper planning, taking into account the environment, can alter a situation such as this.

RECOMMENDATIONS

We would now like to make some recommendations based on our findings and the preceding observations. We note with some satisfaction that our most important recommendation has already been touched upon in the *Final Report* (UNESCO, 1976: p. 16):

> This (structure of education) should be more flexible, and should ensure the redistribution of resources between and the articulation of, school and out-of-school education, reconcile the terminal function and the preparatory role of each level and type of education, and establish closer links between education and the community as well as with the world of work.

(1) Out-of-school education

Our first recommendation is to encourage African countries to pursue vigorously and without delay the modifications in structures of education and the redistribution of resources between school and out-of-school education. It is to be hoped that new structures would result in more efficient and less expensive systems of delivery in schools, with boarding schools (where they exist) giving way to neighbourhood schools. More substantial resources, including the savings from the formal school system, should be ploughed into well thought-out and planned programmes for out-of-school youths which in the rural areas should be made integral components of each country's programme of integrated rural development.

The realities of the African situation would seem to indicate that for some time to come a significant proportion of children in this continent will stay outside the formal school system. If the unhealthy drift into the overcrowded urban areas is to be checked, then African governments must commit themselves to projects which use rural adults and children in symbiotic relationship. At the same time, it should be stated that there is no substitute for improving infrastructural and other facilities in the rural areas of Africa. In Chapter 5 we presented SEPA'S activities in out-of-school education.

(2) Coordinated research on environmental correlates of cognitive functioning of learners

Knowledge of the child in the African setting has been hitherto sketchy and incomplete. Data have been collected in a manner which makes over-all planning difficult. The problem has been lack of coordination on the part of the agencies, institutions and workers who are interested in the affairs of African children, and almost total lack of interest on the part of governments. Also, information has been gathered in certain areas of particular interest to various groups leaving huge gaps in other areas. Obvious as it may seem, planners, teachers, welfare and other workers do not always appear to realize that various facts in the development of children are inextricably interwoven and that successful programmes presuppose a bird's-eye view of the child in his over-all environment. As examples: What is the justification for subjecting the child from the mangrove swamp and the child from a semidesert location to the same educational experience? Should the preventive health care programme not be tailored to suit ecocultural patterns?

In order to collect more useful information for planning and for the development of effective programmes, it is essential that research efforts be coordinated all over the continent and special attention be given to the neglected areas of the child's development and welfare. Since the content and method of teaching should be appropriate to the level of cognitive development reached by the child, there is need to gather basic information about the pace of intellectual development of African children in different environments. In order to develop a broad picture, data are needed from different countries covering various physical and occupational backgrounds, with a wide range of ages in each.

Relevant work is being carried out in several countries, but it is necessary to coordinate these efforts so as to obtain comparable data. To accomplish this coordination a workshop of about two weeks duration could be held for specialists, who should consider in detail, and take the appropriate decisions on, the following issues:

(a)   Which task should be used?
(b)   How shall the tasks be presented?
(c)   How will the samples be drawn?
(d)   How will the results be scored?

In addition to these basic questions, other details of procedure will have to be decided upon. Finally, the participants will have to spend a substantial amount of time practising the administration of the tasks so that they in turn can train others who will join them in carrying out the survey in various locations.

(3) Pre-school education

The third recommendation deals with pre-school education. The explosion in the education of young children in the 1970s presents us with a staggering set of problems, some of which African governments do not seem to fully appreciate. There is a major problem of *intervention* (when and how) to help prepare children for the educational experiences which have been massively embarked upon. Some children come from very poor environmental backgrounds, others are privileged. Yet the teacher, who is not usually well equipped, is expected to deal successfully with the heterogenous group. The problem of intervention has not yet been solved, or even adequately discussed. Different countries in Africa have encouraged the opening of nursery schools but have not established proper agencies, machinery and mechanisms for the supervision of what is done in these schools.

The nursery-school situation is a problematic one. Usually, nursery schools are run by private agencies. These schools need to be supervised. To be really beneficial, studies should be carried out in a number of areas to find out the relationship between school activities and various aspects of child development, such as use of language in instruction (mother tongue or other), the role of various types of materials on concept formation, and social and familial factors that influence attendance and performance in the nursery schools. How can intervention programmes reduce the lag, or stimulate and equip African children to function better in their various environments?

(4) Day-care centres

Our fourth recommendation deals in fact with a specific aspect of pre-school education. In the old African society, the woman who went to the farm or market place had her young children taken care of by older siblings, nurse maids and other relatives. The discovery of education as a powerful weapon of national development is fast changing this situation. On the other hand, the proportion of mothers taking jobs in the productive sectors of the economy is on the increase. It is, therefore, in the interest of society that appropriate arrangements be made for the children of working mothers to be properly cared for when their mothers are at work.

It is pleasing to observe that in at least one country visited this issue was being given deserved attention by the government. A forward-looking government plan was receiving international support, and as a result of the joint venture, day-care centre attendants were being produced for the fast multiplying day-care centres in the country. In addition there was a clearly defined set of criteria put out by government for recognizing day-care centres for aid.

It is suggested to other African governments that the issue of day-care centres deserves and should get serious attention. It might be necessary to organize on the platform of the Organization for African Unity a pan-African workshop on day-care centres. Such a workshop, could, among other things, recommend administrative machinery such as controlling ministry, minimum health and safety requirements and minimum aids and materials necessary for the cognitive and other aspects of development of the children.

(5) Language and thought

The claim may be made that much of the socialization and present-day education of children on the African continent is verbal. Yet, very little is known about the way language actually relates to, and either influences or is influenced by, the thinking of Africans. The problems of language of instruction, sequencing of instruction, the choice and use of official languages, effectiveness of mass communication, as well as language performance in interpersonal situations (teacher—pupil, parent—child, etc.) hinge on the understanding of issues involving language and thought. Mother-tongue education is advocated in some countries, and during FESTAC 77 an African lingua franca was proposed for the whole continent. Clearly workshops and studies are needed to collect information so that realistic policies and plans can be made.

(a) Are the order and process of language universal for African and other children irrespective of environment? Studies could be undertaken from the prelinguistic stage so that the relationship of early interactive acts, prevalence of certain noise factors in the environment, exposure to a variety of languages with various difficulty levels, and language acquisition could be analysed.

(b) Although thought is not altogether limited by the language one speaks, yet the relevance and importance of certain concepts may depend on the availability of modes of expression. Are African children hampered in their education because they possess certain concepts that they cannot express? Or are they hampered in the acquisition of certain concepts by language and usage of mathematical/scientific concepts usually considered "foreign" to Africa?

(c) How can mother-tongue education be introduced and made more effective? What African languages can be used and how can they be expanded to cope with modern education? At what levels should the mother tongue be used in instruction? Well designed research projects and experiments in mother-tongue education should be carried out in various locations. Much emphasis must be given to assessment not just in terms of performance in school work but in over-all cognitive functioning as well.

(d) Studies of language and thought need to be carried out at all levels of development, but particular care should be taken to include older children. Relatively little is known about the language and thought of older children and adolescents and yet they form the group which is subject to formal education.

(e) There should be specific studies of bilingualism. Results of studies have so far been inconclusive (McLaughlin, 1978). Does the learning or usage of more than one language necessarily have a detrimental effect on intellectual development? How can the benefits of bilingualism be maximized?

(6) Classroom practice

The more African governments embark on universal education, the greater the responsibility imposed on teachers at all levels. Services and guidance hitherto provided by families have to be seen to by schools and other agencies. The greater the heterogeneity of pupils, the more difficult and challenging is the task of the teacher. Therefore particular attention has to be given to the selection and pre-service preparation of teachers, to in-service programmes for practising teachers and the production of classroom materials.

(a) Pre-service teacher training institutions should aim at sensitizing trainees to the various levels of development (especially cognitive development) of African children. Their syllabuses should include programmes designed for understanding children as individuals and in small groups. Programmes should also emphasize basic psychological principles which the teacher can use effectively not just for the benefit of pupils, but to generate self-confidence and interest in his own work. Specific skills which are known to be effective in classroom instruction should be taught. For example questioning skills should be developed. How does the teacher ask recall questions, questions demanding synthesis, analysis and application?

(b) Attempts should be made to bring together frequently those responsible for the training of teachers, serving teachers, curriculum developers, and inspectors to discuss and review progress and problems relating to the education of African children. This should be done at various levels — local, national and at the pan-African level. These workshops, meetings or in-service training schemes should involve as much as possible practical work which will challenge the various workers to attempt to solve problems or adapt materials which relate to the changes in the environment or better understanding of African children.

(c) There should be alternative approaches to teacher education to meet special African needs. Some should have the type of built-in innovation exhibited by the Science Education Tutors of the University of Sierra Leone.

(d) Research on the development of instructional materials and learning aids in different subject areas is required.

(e) There should be detailed exploration of the demands of the curriculum on the child's intellectual level. This could be done on the basis of individual subjects or related topics.

(f) Specialists in various disciplines and levels of education need to be trained. There is still a shortage of manpower in most countries.

(7) The environmental component of education

Our seventh recommendation deals with the environmental component of education. The education of the child must be such that it will enable him to understand his environment, know how to use it properly and secure a measure of control over it. In Africa, at present there is a tendency toward the misuse of the environment. One way to reverse this trend is through appropriate environmental education. This suggests paying adequate attention to the environmental component of education in the planning and execution of all school and out-of-school curricula. It also suggests appropriate training of teachers.

In all of these respects, there is need for African countries to develop proper channels for exchanging information among themselves and with other nations. The role that several agencies and organs of the United Nations and most especially the United Nations Environmental Programme (UNEP) can play in this connection should be under-scored.

(8) International cooperation on matters relating to children

Our eighth recommendation is that international cooperation on matters relating to children should be encouraged more than is now the case. In this respect African countries may wish to set up a permanent commission on children on the platform of the Organization for African Unity (OAU). Such a commission could use specialists in universities and other institutions to collect and collate data on children in various parts of Africa. Channels for disseminating such information to Member States of the OAU as well as to other parts of the world could also be devised. Finally, it should be able to synthesize information available on children other than those in OAU Member States, for use in Africa.

APPENDIX 1 SOME STATISTICS ON COUNTRIES SURVEYED

Country	Estimated Population 1975	Population Growth Rate 1963–72 (%)	Pupils Enrolled for First-Level Education in Year Shown	Teaching Staff for First-Level Education In Year Shown	Pupils Enrolled for Second Level Education in Year Shown	Teaching Staff for Second Level Education in Year Shown
Botswana	691,000	2.8	116,293 (1975)	3,509 (1975)	14,286 (1975)	860 (1975)
Ghana	9,866,000	2.9	1,051,012 (1974)	33,334 (1974)	531,966 (1974)	22,759 (1974)
Ivory Coast	4,885,000	2.4	641,369 (1974)	14,403 (1974)	103,642 (1974)	4,579 (1974)
Kenya	13,339,000	3.1	2,881,155 (1975)	86,107 (1975)	235,501 (1975)	9,730 (1975)
Liberia	1,039,000 (UNESCO) 1,938,000 (IPPF, 1970)	1.7	157,821 (1975)	3,832 (1975)	34,151 (1975)	1,016 (1970)
Mauritius	899,000	1.9 (1973)	152,417 (1974)	5,568 (1974)	62,015 (1974)	2,027 (1974)
Nigeria	62,925,000 (UNESCO) 79,758,969 (IPPF, 1973)	2.5	4,662,400 (1973)	136,142 (1973)	544,520 (1974)	20,448 (1973)
Senegal	4,136,000	2.4	283,276 (1972)	6,159 (1972)	59,401 (1970)	—
Sierra Leone	2,707,000 (1974)	1.5	189,657 (1974)	5,993 (1974)	47,614 (1974)	1,629 (1974)
United Republic of Tanzania	15,300,000	2.6	1,591,834 (1975)	29,783 (1975)	63,187 (1975)	3,218 (1975)
Upper Volta	6,032,000	2.1	132,825 (1974)	2,904 (1974)	15,470 (1974)	757 (1974)
Zaire	24,902,000	3.9	3,292,020 (1972)	80,481 (1972)	335,203 (1973)	14,483 (1973)
Zambia	4,896,000	2.6	858,191 (1974)	17,881 (1974)	70,974 (1974)	1,144 (1965)

83

APPENDIX 2 ESTIMATED POPULATIONS OF CHILDREN IN SUB-SAHARAN AFRICA

Age groups in years	Population 1970	Population 1975
0–4	39,846,000	47,345,000
5–9	32,412,000	39,717,000
10–14	27,470,000	31,056,000
15–19	23,443,000	26,638,000

(Source: UNESCO Yearbook, 1976)

APPENDIX 3   INTELLECTUAL DEVELOPMENT

TABLE 1 CONSERVATION TASKS

Country	Authors	Testing Situation +	Tasks ++	Modified	Sample	Age Range	Background of Students	Comments (* indicates positive effect)
Senegal	Greenfield (1966)	1	Q(l)	No	187	6–13	Urban/rural	*age; *schooling; rural urban
Sierra Leone	Kamara (1971) Kamara and Easley (1977)	4	Q(s),W,V	No	55	6–12	Schooled un-schooled	*schooling (slight); *age
Sierra Leone	Ohuche (1971)	5	N,W	Yes	231	5–8	Town-village	*age; independent of location
Ghana	Beard (1968)	5	Q(s)	No	240	7–14	Urban	individual scores not reported
Ghana	Fitzgerald (1970)	5	Q(s),L	Yes	413	5–11	Urban/suburban/rural	*age; *schooling; *suburban (except Q(s))
Ghana	Ayisi (1972)	4	Q(l,s),N,A	No	74	5–12	Univ./primary school	*age; no sex difference
Ghana	Adjei (1973; 1977)	4	Q(l,s),N,W,V	No	76	7–9	Rural/elite	*specific experiences; *maternal behaviour
Nigeria	Prince-Williams (1961)	1	Q(s),N	Yes	45	5–8	Rural, unschooled	*age
Nigeria	Poole (1968)	5	Q(l,s),W	Yes	150	10–11	Urban/village/rural	English; urban/village/rural
Nigeria	Etuk (1967)	4	N	No	110	6–8	Traditional/modern	male/female; modern/traditional
Nigeria	Lloyd (1971 a,b)	5	Q(l),N	No	80	3,5–8	Urban	*age; elite/traditional
Nigeria	Owoc (1973)	5	Q(l)	Yes	449	6–over 18	Varied	urban/rural; schooled/unschooled
Rwanda	Pinard et al. (1973)	5	Q(l,s)	No	64	6–8	Rural; schooled/not	training effective; no group differences
Uganda	Vernon (1969)	2	Q(l,s)L,A,V	Yes	50	11	Urban boys	below Jamaican, British
Uganda	Almy et al. (1970)	5	Q(l),N	No	64	5–11	Urban	some improvement with years in school
Uganda	Okonji (1971a)	5	L	Yes	300	6–16	Not urban	*age; *schooling
Uganda	Otaala (1971a,b)	4	Q(l,s),N	No	160	6–12	Rural	*age
Uganda	Otaala (1971c)	5	Q(l,s),N	No	91	Adults	Unschooled	lower than children
Uganda	Otaala (1972)	5	Q(l,s),N	No	678	6–13	5 ethnic groups	*age
Uganda	Goldschmid et al. (1973)	5	Q(l,s),N,W,A	No	198	5–8	Rural	*age
Nigeria	Omotoso (1975)	–	N,L,V	–	120	4–8	Urban	Strong correlation with mathematics achievement

TABLE 1 (contd.)

Country	Authors	Testing + Situation	Tasks ++	Modified	Sample	Age Range	Background of Students	Comments (* indicates positive effect)
Nigeria	Duruji (1975)	4	Q(s),N, L,W,V	Yes	200	6–10	Rural	*age; conservation achieved at same age as in other societies
Rwanda	Laurendeau (1977)	5	N,A	No	559	5–12	Schooled/ partially Schooled/ unschooled	*age; *schooling; lag with Montreal group
Kenya	Mureria and Okatcha (1977)	4	L,A,V	No	120	7–12	Rural	*age; *male lag with Swiss norms
Ivory Coast	Dasen, Lavallée and Retschitzki (1979)	2/1a	Q(e,s)N	No	73	7–14	Rural	*training, generalized to other concepts, bridged time lag
Ivory Coast	Dasen (1975)	2	Q,W,V	No	40	8–14	Rural	*age; conservation space concepts
Nigeria	Fahrmeler (1978)	5	N,L,Q (e,s) A	No	449	5–15	town/village schooled/non-schooled	*age; *schooling, social class and sex on same tasks only; village town on same tasks
Mali	Dena Siancoumbe	4	Q(l,s),N,L	Yes	405	6–9	Urban/rural	small effect of urbanization no significant difference with Western studies
Kenya	Kiminyo (1973;1977)	4	Q(s),W,V	No	120	7–12	Urban/rural	no difference for schooling, urbanization, sex
Tanzania	Nyiti (1973;1977)	4	Q(s)W,V	No	139	8–14	Schooled/ unschooled	*age; no difference for schooling
Zambia	Heron and Simonsson (1969)	3	W	Yes	336	5–17	Urban	*age; European/African after 10 years
Zambia	MacArthur (1973)	?	Q(l,s),L,A,V	?	192	9–40	Varied	results not reported
Rhodesia	Hendrikz (1966)	1a	Q(s),N	?	304	5	Urban	*nursery school; European/African

+Key to testing situation
1. Foreign tests in local language
1a. Foreign tests with interpreter
2. Foreign tests in English
3. Foreign tests, non-verbal method
4. Originator of experiment tested in local language
5. Originator of experiment trained indigenous testers

++Key to conservation tasks
Q(l) = liquid quantity
Q(s) = solid substance (continuous and discontinuous)
W = weight
V = volume by displacement
N = number
L = length
A = area

TABLE 2 CLASSIFICATION

Country	Reference	Method	Findings
Senegal	Greenfield et al. (1966)	Free sorting; constrained sorting	*schooling; colour > form or function
Sierra Leone	Kamara (1971)	Free sorting	both schooled and unschooled Ss can abstract
Liberia	Irwin and McLaughlin (1970)	Constrained sorting	*age; colour > form
Liberia	Cole et al. (1971)	Free, constrained; oddity problem	*schooling; different factors determine classificatory behaviour
Nigeria	Prince-Williams (1962)	Free sorting; oddity problem	*age
Nigeria	Etuk (1967)	Free sorting, class inclusion	*age; class inclusion more difficult than conservation
Nigeria	Kellaghan (1968)	Free sorting, constrained sorting	modern > traditional on many; colour > form
Nigeria	Okonji (1970)	Free sorting	*training
Nigeria	Okonji (1971 b)	Free sorting	*age; European = African
Nigeria	Lloyd (1971 a)	Oddity problem	modern > traditional
Uganda	Vernon (1969)	Free sorting	below Jamaican, British
Uganda	Almy et al. (1970)	Free sorting; constrained sorting	colour > form; abstraction increases with age
Uganda	Otaala (1971 a,b)	Free sorting; class inclusion	class inclusion more difficult than conservation
Kenya	Fjellman (1969)	Free sorting	abstraction aided by locally relevant system
Zambia	Serpell (1969 a,b)	Oddity problem	colour > form: form choice increases with age
Zambia	Deregowski and Serpell (1971)	Constrained sorting	European > African; pictures not equivalent to objects
Rhodesia	Hendrikz (1966)	Class inclusion	more difficult than conservation, easier than seriation
Nigeria	Omotoso (1975)	Classification	Strong correlation with mathematics achievement
Ivory Coast	Lavallée and Dasen (1979)	Class inclusion (7–9 years)	*training, generalized to conservation
Ivory Coast	Tapé (1977)	Free sorting, class inclusion and intersection	urban/rural tested in French or vernacular *interaction content/Language
Kenya	Dasen, Lavallée and Ngini (1979)	Class inclusion (12–14 years)	*training: "actualization"

87

REFERENCES

Adjei, K. (1973) *Maternal Behaviours and Cognitive Development.* Unpublished Ph.D. thesis, University of Strathclyde.

Adjei, K. (1977) Influence of specific maternal occupation and behaviour on Piagetian cognitive development. In P. R. Dasen (Ed.), *Piagetian Psychology: Cross Cultural Contributions.* Gardner Press, New York. pp. 227–256.

Ainsworth, M. D. (1967) *Infancy in Uganda: Infant Care and the growth of love.* Johns Hopkins University Press, Baltimore, Md.

Albino, R. C., and V. J. Thompson (1956) The effects of sudden weaning on Zulu children. *Brit. J. Med. Psych., 29,* pp. 177–210.

Almy, M., J. Davitz, and M. A. White (1970) *Studying School Children in Uganda: Four Reports of Exploratory Research.* Teachers College Press, New York.

Anastasi, A. (1958) *Differential Psychology: Individual and Group Differences in Behaviour.* MacMillan Co., New York.

Ashton, H. (1952) *The Basuto.* Oxford Univ. Press, New York.

Ayisi, C. H. (1972) *Performance of Ghanaian Children on Some Piagetian Conservation Tasks.* Research Report, School of Education, University of Cape Coast.

Baga Yoko, M. (1978) La maîtrise des opérations formelles par les ruraux de Kita, adultes alphabétisés en Bambara et adultes analphabètes. Memoire inédit, E. N. S., Bamako, Mali.

Bayley, N. (1969) *Bayley Scales of Infant development.* Psychological Corporation, New York.

Beard, R. M. (1968) An Investigation into Mathematical Concepts among Ghanaian Children. *Teach. Educ. New Countries, 9,* pp. 3–14, 132–145.

Berry, J. W. (1966) Temne and Eskimo perceptual skills. *International J. of Psychology, 1, 3,* 207–229.

Berry, J. W. (1974) Radical cultural relativism and the concept of intelligence. In J. W. Berry and P. R. Dasen (Eds.), *Culture and cognition: readings in cross-cultural psychology.* Methuen, London. pp. 225–230.

Berry, J. W. (1976) *Human ecology and cognitive style: comparative studies in cultural and psychology adaptation.* Wiley, New York.

Biesheuvel, S. (1959) The nature of intelligence: some practical implications of its measurements. *Psygram, 1, 6,* 78–80. Reprinted in J. W. Berry and P. R. Dasen (Eds.), *Culture and Cognition.* Methuen, London. 1974, pp. 221–224.

Bisilliat, J., D. Laya, E. Pierre, and Ch. Pidoux (1967) La notion de Lakkal dans la culture Djerma – Songhai. *Psychopathologie Africaine, 3, 2,* pp. 209–222.

Bovet, M. C., P. R. Dasen, and B. Inhelder (1974) Etapes de l'intelligence sensori-motrice chez l'enfant Baoulé: Etude préliminaire. *Archives de Psychologie*, 41, Vol. 1972, pp. 164, 363–386.

Bower, T. G. R. (1974a) *Development in Infancy*, Freeman, Reading.

Bower, T. G. R. (1974b) Competent newborns. *New Scientist*, 61, 889, pp. 672–5.

Brunet, O., and I. Lézine (1951) *Le développement psychologique de la première enfance.* 3e édition, 1971, P. U. F., Paris.

Casati, I., and I. Lézine (1968) *Les étapes de l'intelligence sensorimotrice. Manuel.* Centre de psychologie appliquée, Paris.

Christiansen, N., I. Vouri, J. O. Mora, and M. Wagner (1974) Social environment as it relates to malnutrition and mental development. In J. Cravioto, L. Hambraeus, and B. Vahlquist (Eds.), *Early malnutrition and mental development.* Almqvist and Wiksell, Stockholm. pp. 186–199.

Cole, M., J. Gay, J. A. Glick, and D. W. Sharp (1971) *The Cultural Context of Learning and Thinking.* Methuen, London.

Cole, M., and S. Scribner (1974) *Culture and Thought: a psychological introduction.* John Wiley, New York.

Cole, M., and S. Scribner (1977) Developmental theories applied to cross-cultural cognitive research. *Annals of the N. Y. Acad. Sc.,* 285, pp. 366–373.

Corman and Escalona (1969) Stages in sensory motor development: replication study. Merril Palmer Quarterly, 15, 4, pp. 351–361.

Cravioto, J., and B. Robles (1965) Evolution of adaptive and motor behaviour during rehabilitation from kwashiorkor. *Amer. J. Orthop.,* 35, pp. 449–464.

Dague, P. (1970a) *Psychologie de l'enfant et de l'adolescent en Afrique et à Madagascar.* AUDECAM, Paris.

Dague, P. (1970b) *Bibliographie analytique des recherches effectuées sur l'enfant Africain francophone.* Abidjan, Ministère de l'Education Nationale, Programme d'éducation télevisuelle.

Dasen, P. R. (1974) Le développement du jeune enfant africain. *Archives de Psychologie,* 41, Vol. 1972, 164, pp. 341–361.

Dasen, P. R. (1974) Concrete Operational development in three cultures. *J. Cross-cultural Psych.,* 6, 2, pp. 156–172.

Dasen, P. R. (1977a) Are cognitive processes universal? a contribution to cross-cultural psychology. In N. Warren (Ed.), *Studies in cross-cultural Psychology* Vol. I. Academic Press, London.

Dasen, P. R. (1977b) Cross-Cultural Cognitive development. The cultural aspects of Piaget's theory. In Issues in cross-cultural research. *Annals of the New York Academy of Sciences,* 285, pp. 322–340.

Dasen, P. R., J. W. Berry, and H. Witkin (1979) The use of development theories cross-culturally. In L. Eckensberger, Y. Poortinga and W. Lonner (Eds.), *Applied cross-cultural research and the development of psychological science.* Swets and Zeitlinger, Amsterdam.

Dasen, P. R., M. Lavallée, and L. Ngini (1979) Cross-cultural training studies of concrete operations. In L. Eckensberger, Y. Poortinga and W. Looner (Eds.), *Applied cross-cultural research and the development of psychological science.* Swets and Zeitlinger, Amstredam.

Dasen, P. R., M. Lavallée, and J. Retschitzki (1979) Training conservation of quality (liquids) in West African (Baoulé) children. *Intern. J. of Psychol.,* 14, in press.

Dasen, P. R., B. Inhelder, M. Lavallée and J. Retschitzki (1978) *Naissance de l'intelligence chez l'enfant Baoulé de Côte d'Ivoire.* Hans Huber, Berne.

Dasen, P. R., M. Lavallée, J. Retschitzki and M. Reinhardt (1977) Early malnutrition and the development of sensori-motor intelligence. *J. Trop. Pediatrics and Environmental Child Health*, 23, 3, pp. 146–157, and in F. M. Okatcha (Ed.), *Modern Psychology and Cultural Adaptation*. Swahili Language Consultants and publishers, Nairobi. pp. 3–25.

Davids, A., R. H. Holden, and G. B. Gray (1963) Maternal anxiety during pregnancy and adequacy of mother and child adjustment eight months following childbirth. *Child development*, 34, pp. 993–1002.

de Lemos, M. M. (1969) The Development of Conservation in Aboriginal Children. *Int. J. Psychol.*, 4, pp. 255–269.

de Lemos, M. M. (1974) The development of spatial concepts in Zulu children. In J. W. Berry and P. R. Dasen (Eds.), *Culture and cognition: readings in cross-cultural psychology*. Methuen, London. 367–380.

Dena Siancoumbé, J. G. (1977) Etude comparative des citadins scolarisés (de Bamako) et des ruraux scolarisés (de Tominian), niveau des opérations concrètes. Mémoire inédit, E. N. S., Bamako, Mali.

Deregowski, J. B. and R. Serpell (1971) Performance on a Sorting Task. A Cross-cultural Experiment. *Int. J. Psychol.*, 6, pp. 273–281.

Diakite, S. (1978) Maîtrise des opérations formelles. Etude comparative entre adolescents scolarisés et non-scolarisés de la région de Kayes. Memoire inédit, E. N. S., Bamako, Mali.

Dubowitz, L., V. Dubowitz, and C. Goldberg (1970) Clinical assessment of gestational age in the newborn infant. *J. Pediatrics*, 77, pp. 1–10.

Durojaiye, M. O. A. (1976) *A New Introduction to Educational Psychology*. Evans Brothers Limited, London.

Duruji, C. A. (1975) Conservation acquisition: Piaget's formulation examined in Ibo-speaking Nigerian children. Unpubl. Ph.D. thesis, Univ. of Ibadan.

Erny, P. (1968) *L'enfant dans la pensée traditionelle de l'Afrique noire*. Le livre Africain, Paris.

Erny, P. (1972a) *L'enfant et son milieu en Afrique Noire, Essais sur l'éducation traditionelle*. Payot, Paris.

Erny, P. (1972b) *Les premiers pas dans la vie de l'enfant d'Afrique noire. Naissance et première enfance. Eléments pour une ethnologie de l'éducation*. l'Ecole, Paris.

Etuk, E. E. S. (1967) *The Development of Number Concepts: An Examination of Piaget's Theory with Yoruba-speaking Nigerian Children*. Unpublished Ph.D thesis, Columbia University.

Evans, J. L. (1970) *Children in Africa*. Teachers College, Columbia University, New York.

Fahrmeier, E. D. (1975) The development of concrete operations among the Hausa. *J. Cross-Cult. Psychol.*, 9, 1, pp. 23–44.

Ferreira, A. J. (1960) The pregnant woman's emotional attitude and its reflection on the newborn. *Am J. of Orthopsychiatry*, 30, pp. 553–561.

Fitzgerald, L. K. (1970) *Cognitive Development among Ga Children: Environmental Correlates of Cognitive Growth Rate within the Ga Tribe*. Unpublished Ph.D. thesis, University of California, Berkeley.

Fjellman, J. (1969) Methods of Investigating Cognitive Development of Children in Rural Kenya: Some Kamba Results, (Mimographed). Bureau of Educational Research, University of Nairobi.

Flavell, J. (1963) *The Developmental Psychology of Jean Piaget*. Van Nostrand Reinhold Co., New York.

Gabbud, J. P., K. A. Gbedemah, G. P. Ravelli, S. Herzen, Cl. Meylan, and A. von Muralt (1975) Biochemical study on the nutritional status of children in the Ivory Coast. *Proc. 9th. Int. Congr. Nutr. Mexico 1972*, 4, pp. 128–132. Karger, Basel.

Gay, J. and Cole, M. (1967) *The New mathematics and an old culture*. Holt, Rinehart and Winston, New York.

Geber, M., and R. F. A. Dean (1957) The state of development of newborn African children. *Lancet*, 272, pp. 1216–1219.

Gesell, A. and C. Amatruda (1947) *Developmental Diagnosis*. Harper Brothers, New York.

Goldberg, S. (1972) Infant care and growth in urban Zambia. *Human Development*, 15, pp. 77–89.

Goldschmid, M. L., *et al.* (1973) A Cross-cultural Investigation of Conservation. *J. Cross-cult. Psychol.*, 4, pp. 75–88.

Greenfield, P. M. (1966) On Culture and Conservation. In J. S. Bruner, R. R. Olver, and P. M. Greenfield (Eds.), *Studies in Cognitive Growth*. Wiley, New York. pp. 225–256.

Greenfield, P. M., L. C. Reich, and R. R. Olver (1966) On Culture and Equivalence: II. J. S. Bruner, R. R. Olver, and P. M. Greenfield (Eds.), *Studies in Cognitive Growth*. Wiley, New York. pp. 270–318.

Griffiths, J. McE. (1969) Development of reflexes in Bantu children. *Developmental Medicine and Child Neurology*, 11, pp. 533–535.

Griffiths, R. (1970) *The abilities of young children. A comprehensive system of mental measurement for the first 8 years of life*. Young and Sons, London.

Guyler, K. R. (1969) *The effects of some Task and Subject Variables on the Accuracy and Process of Seriation of Length: A Comparison between Infant and Junior Children Based on the Original Work of Jean Piaget*. Unpublished M.A. (Education) Thesis, University of London.

Hendrikz, E. (1966) *A cross-cultural Investigation of the Number Concepts and Level of Number Development in Five-year-old Urban Shona and European Children in Southern Rhodesia*. Unpublished M.A. (Psychology) Thesis, University of London.

Heron, A. (1971) Concrete Operations, 'g', and Achievement in Zambian Children. *J. cross-cult. Psychol.*, 2, pp. 325–336.

Heron, A., and M. Simonsson (1969) Weight Conservation in Zambian Children: a non-verbal Approach. *Int. J. Psychol.*, 4, pp. 281–292.

Hertzig, M. E., H. G. Birch, S. A. Richardson, and J. Tizard (1972) Intellectual levels of school children severely malnourished during the first two years of life. *Pediatrics*, 49, pp. 814–824.

Hoorweg, J. C. (1976) *Protein-energy malnutrition and intellectual abilities. A study of teen-age Ugandan children*. Mouton, The Hague.

Ingle, R. B., and M. Shayer (1971) Conceptual Demands in Nuffield O-level Chemistry. *Educ. Chem.* 8, pp. 182–183.

Inhelder, B., and J. Piaget (1964) *The Early Growth of Logic in the Child*. Routledge and Kegan Paul, London.

Inhelder, B., H. Sinclair, and M. Bovet (1974) *Les structures de la connaissance: apprentissage et developpement*. P. U. F., Paris.

(1974) *Learning and the development of cognition*. Harvard Univ. Press, Cambridge, Mass.

Irwin, H. M., and D. H. McLaughlin (1970) Ability and Preference in Category Sorting by Mano School Children and Adults. *J. Soc. Psychol.*, 82, pp. 15–24.

Jahoda, G., J. B. Deregowski, and D. Sinha (1974) Topological and Euclidean spatial features noted by children: A cross-cultural study. *Int. J. Psychol.*, 9, 3, pp. 159–172.

Jelliffe, D. B. (1966) *The assessment of the nutritional status of the community.* WHO Monogr. Series, no. 53. French translation: *Appréciation de l'état nutritionnel des populations.* Monographie no. 53, OMS, 1969.

Kallaghan, T. P. (1968) Abstraction and Categorisation in African Children. *Int. J. Psychol.,* 3, pp. 115–150.

Kamara, A. A. (1971) *Cognitive Development among School Age Themne Children of Sierra Leone.* Unpublished Ph.D. Thesis, University of Illinois, Urbana-Champaign, Ill.

Kamara, A. A., and J. A. Easley, Jr. (1977) Is the rate of cognitive development uniform across cultures? A methodological critique with new evidence from Themne children. In P. R. Dasen (Ed.), *Piagetian Psychology: Cross-cultural contributions.* Gardner Press (Halsted, Wiley), New York. pp. 26–63.

Kidd, A. H. and J. L. Rivoire (1965) The culture-fair aspects of the development of spatial perceptions, *Journal of Genetic Psychology,* 106, pp. 101–111.

Kihm, J. M. and G. Tapé (1977) Le langage des amulettes en pays M'batto, *Ann. Univ. Abidjan,* série D, 10, pp. 123–152.

Kilbride, P. L. (1977) Early psycho-motor development and cultural practices among the Samia. Paper presented to Inst. of African Studies, Univ. of Nairobi, Aug. 1977.

Kilbride, P. L., and J. E. Kilbride (1974) Sociocultural factors and the early manifestation of sociability behaviour among Baganda infants. *Ethos,* pp. 296–314.

Kilbride, J. E. and P. L. Kilbride (1975) Sitting and smiling behaviour of Baganda infants: The influence of culturally-constituted experience. *J. of Cross-cultural Psychol.,* 6, 1, pp. 88–107.

Kiminyo, D. M. (1973) *A Cross-cultural Study of the Development of Conservation of Mass, Weight, and Volume in Kenyan Children.* Unpublished Ph.D. Thesis, University of Alberta.

Kiminyo, D. M. (1977) A cross-cultural study of the development of conservation of mass, weight, and volume among Kamba children. In P. R. Dasen (Ed.), *Piagetian psychology: cross-cultural contributions.* Gardner Press, New York. pp. 64–88.

Kirk, L. (1975) Estimating the ages of children in nonliterate populations: a field method. *J. of Cross-cultural Psychol.,* 6, 2, pp. 238–249.

Kirk, L. (1977) Maternal and subcultural correlates of cognitive growth rate: the Ga pattern. In P. R. Dasen (Ed.), *Piagetian Psychology: Cross-cultural contributions.* Gardner Press, New York. pp. 257–295.

Klein, R. E., C. Yarbrough, R. E. Lasky, and J. P. Habicht (1974) Correlations of mild to moderate protein-calorie malnutrition among rural Guatemalan infants and preschool children. In J. Cravioto, L. Hambraeus and B. Vahlquist (Eds.), *Early malnutrition and mental development.* Almquist and Wiksell, Stockholm. pp. 168–181.

Kline, P. (1977) Cross-cultural studies and Freudian theory. In N. Warren (Ed.). *Studies in cross-cultural psychology,* Vol. I, Academic Press, London. pp. 51–90.

Knappen, M. T. (1962) *L'enfant Mukongo.* Nauwelaerts, Louvain.

Konner, M. J. (1972) Aspects of the developmental ethology of a foraging people. In N. Blurton-Jones (Ed.), *Ethological studies of child behaviour.* Cambridge University Press, London. pp. 285–304.

Kopp, C. B., and M. Sigman (1972) UCLA revision of the administration manual: the stages of sensory-motor intelligence in the child from birth to two years by Irène Casati and Irène Lézine. Unpubl. manuscript.

Kopp, C. B., M. Sigman, and A. H. Parmelee (1974) A longitudinal study of sensori-motor development. *Developmental Psychology,* 10, pp. 687–695.

REFERENCES 93

Laurendeau-Bendavid, M. (1977) Culture, schooling and cognitive development: a comparative study of children in French Canada and Rwanda. In P. R. Dasen (Ed.), *Piagetian Psychology: Cross-cultural contributions*. Gardner Press, New York. pp. 123–168.

Lautrey, J., and H. R. Tomé (1976) Etudes interculturelles de la notion de conservation. In M. Reuchlin (Ed.), *Cultures et conduites*. P. U. F., Paris. pp. 247–281.

Lavallée, M., and P. R. Dasen (1979) L'apprentissage de la notion d'inclusion de classes chez de jeunes enfants Baoulés (Côte d'Ivoire). *J. Intern. de Psychol.*, 14, in press.

Le Vine, R. A. (1973) *Culture, behaviour and personality*. Aldine, Chicago.

Lewis, M. (1976) *Origins of intelligence. Infancy and early childhood*. Plenum Press, New York.

Lézine, I., N. Stambak, and I. Casati (1969) *Les étapes de l'intelligence sensori-motorice. Monographie No. I.*

Lloyd, B. B. (1971a) The Intellectual Development of Yoruba Children: a Re-Examination, *J. cross-cult. Psychol.*, 2, 29–38.

Lloyd, B. B. (1971b) Studies of conservation with Yoruba Children at Differing Ages and Experience. *Child Dev.*, 42, pp. 415–428.

Lloyd, B. B. (1972) *Perception and cognition from a cross-cultural perspective*. Penguin, London.

Lovell, K. and A. Slater (1960) The Growth of the Concept of Times: A Comparative study. *J. Child Psychol. Psychiat.*, 1, pp. 179–190.

MacArthur, R. (1973) Some Ability Patterns: Central Eskimos and Nsenga Africans. *Int. J. Psychol.*, 8, pp. 239–247.

McLaughlin, B. (1978) *Second-language Acquisition in childhood*. Lawrence Elbaum Association Publishers, Hillsdale, N. J.

McLaren, D. S., and W. W. C. Read (1972) Classification of nutritional status in early childhood. *The Lancet*, 2 July 1972, pp. 146–148.

Mmari, G. R. V., (1974) *Tanzania's Experience in and Efforts to Resolve the Problems of Teaching Mathematics through a Foreign Language*, UNESCO, ED-74/CONF.808.

Modgil, S., and C. Modgil (1976) *Piagetian Research: Compilation and Commentary*. N. F. E. R., Windsor.

Mora, J. O. *et al.* (1974) Nutrition, health and social factors related to intellectual performance. *World Review of Nutrition and Dietetics*, 19, pp. 205–236.

Morley, D. (1973) *Paediatric priorities in the developing world*. Butterworth, London. Traduction française: *Pédiatrie dans les pays en développement: Problèmes prioritaires*. Flammarion, Paris. 1977.

Mundy-Castle, A. C. (1976) *Psychology and the search for meaning*. Unpubl. manuscript. Univ. of Lagos.

Mundy-Castle, A. C. (1978) Looking strategies in infants – a cross-cultural study. Paper presented to the 4th International I. A. C. C. P. Congress, Munich, July–Aug. 1978.

Mundy-Castle, A. C., and M. O. Okonji (1976) *Mother-infant interaction in Nigeria*. Manuscript, Dept. of Psychology, Univ. of Lagos, July 1976.

Munroe, R. L., and R. H. Munroe (1975) *Cross-cultural human development*. Brooks–Cole, Monterey, Calif.

Mureria, M. and F. M. Okatcha (1977) Conservation of concepts of length, area and volume among Kikuyu primary school children. In F. M. Okatcha (Ed.), *Modern psychology and cultural adaptation*. Swahili Language Consultants and Publishers, Nairobi. pp. 26–38.

Nyiti, R. M. (1973) *Intellectual Development in the Meru Children of Tanzania*. Unpublished Ph.D. Thesis, University of Illinois, Urbana-Champaign, Ill.

Nyiti, R. M. (1977) The development of conservation among the Meru children of Tanzania. In F. M. Okatcha (Ed.) *Modern psychology and cultural adaptation.* Swahili Language Consultants and Publishers, Nairobi. pp. 59–84.

Ohuche, R. O. (1971) Piaget and the Mende of Sierra Leone, *J. Exp. Educ.,* **39,** pp. 75–78.

Ohuche, R. O (1972) *The Uses of Real Numbers in Traditional Sierra Leone,* Mimeographed. Library, Njala University College.

Ohuche, R. O (1973) Geometry, Estimation and Measurement in Traditional Sierra Leone. *Report of Research in Commonwealth Countries.* Education Division, Commonwealth Secretariat, London.

Ohuche, R. O. and R. E. Pearson (1974) Piaget and Africa: A survey of research involving conservation and classification in Africa. In *Final Report. Seminar on the Development of Science and Mathematics Concepts in Young Children in African Countries.* UNESCO–UNICEF, Nairobi. pp. 43-59.

Okatcha, F. M. (1977) In F. M. Okatcha (Ed.), *Modern Psychology and Cultural Adaptation.* Swahili Language Consultants and Publishers, Nairobi.

Okeke, E. A. C. (1976) *A study of the understanding in Nigerian School Certificate Biology candidates of the concept of Reproduction, Transport Mechanisms and Growth.* Unpublished Ph.D. Thesis, University of Leeds.

Okonji, M. O. (1970) The Effect of Special Training on the Classificatory Behaviour of Some Nigerian Ibo Children. *Br. J. Educ. Psychol.,* **40,** pp. 21–26.

Okonji, M. O. (1971a) Culture and Children's Understanding of Geometry. *Int. J. Psychol.,* **6,** pp. 121–128.

Okonji, M. O. (1971b) A Cross-Cultural Study of the Effects of Familiarity on Classificatory Behaviour. *J. Cross-cult. Psychol.,* **2,** pp. 39–49.

Okonji, M. O. (in press) Cognitive styles across cultures. In N. Warren (Ed.), *Studies in Cross-cultural Psychology, Vol. 2.* Academic Press, London.

Omari, I. M. (1975) Developmental order of spatial concepts among primary school children in Tanzania. *J. Cross-Cult. Psych.,* **6, 4,** pp. 444–456.

Omari, I. M. (1977) Cognitive egocentricism: age and environmental variables in spatial decentration among Tanzanian children. In F. M. Okatcha (Ed.), *Modern psychology and cultural adaptation.* Swahili Language Consultants and Publishers, Nairobi. pp. 59–84.

Omotoso, H. M. (1976) Conservation, seriation, classification and mathematics achievement in Nigerian children. *Psychol. Reports,* **38,** p. 1335.

Otaala, B. (1971a) *The Development of Operational Thinking in Primary School Children: An Examination of Some Aspects of Piaget's Theory among the Iteso Children of Uganda.* Unpublished Ed.D. Thesis, Columbia University.

Otaala, B. (1971b) *The Development of Operational Thinking in Primary School Children.* Teachers College Press, New York.

Otaala, B. (1971c) A Preliminary Investigation of the Conservation Abilities of Unschooled Iteso Adults. *Uganda J.,* **35,** (1), 63–67.

Otaala, B. (1971c) The Classification Ability of Unschooled Rural Iteso Adults. *Uganda J.,* **35** (2), pp. 189–194.

Otaala, B. (1972) *Conservation Abilities of Primary School Children in Five Ethnic Areas of Uganda,* Makerere University, Faculty of Education, Kampala.

Ottinger, D. R., and J. E. Simmons (1964) Behaviour of human neonates and prenatal maternal anxiety. *Psychological Reports,* **14,** pp. 391–394.

Owoc, P. J. (1973) On Culture and Conservation Once Again, *Int. J. Psychol.,* **8,** pp. 249–254.

Page, H. W. (1973) Concepts of length and distance in a study of Zulu youths. *J. of Soc. Psych.,* 90, pp. 9–16.

Piaget, J., and B. Inhelder (1948) *La représentation de l'espace chez l'enfant.* P. U. F. Paris. Translation: *The child's conception of space.* Routledge and Kegan Paul, London (1956).

Piaget, J. (1966) Nécessité et signification des recherches comparatives en psychologie genetique. *Int. J. Psychol.,* 1, pp. 3–13.

Pinard, A., C. Norin, and M. Le Febvre (1973) Apprentissage de la conservation des quantités liquides chez des enfants rwandais et canadiens-français, *Int. J. Psychol.,* 8, pp. 15–23.

Poole, H. E. (1968) The Effect of Urbanization upon Scientific Concept Attainment among the Hausa Children of Northern Nigeria, *Br. J. educ. Psychol.,* 38, pp. 57–63.

Pratoomraj, S. and R. C. Johnson (1966) Kinds of Questions and Types of Conservation Tasks as Related to Children's Conservation Responses, *Child Dev.,* 37, pp. 343–353.

Price-Williams, D. R. A. (1961) A study Concerning Concepts of Conservation of Quantity among Primitive Children, *Acta Psychol.,,* 18, pp. 297–305.

Price-Williams, D. R. A. (1962) Abstract and Concrete Modes of Classification in a Primitive Society, *Br. J. Educ. Psychol.,* 32, pp. 50–61.

Price-Williams, D. R. (Ed.) (1969) *Cross-cultural studies,* Penguin books, London.

Price-Williams, D. R. (1975) *Explorations in cross-cultural psychology.* Chandler and Sharp, San Francisco.

Rebelsky, F., and P. A. Daniel (1976) Cross-cultural studies of infant intelligence. In M. Lewis (Ed.) *Origins of intelligence,* Plenum Press, New York. pp. 279–288.

Reinhardt, M. C., R. Gautier, and N. Reinhardt (in press) A study of 204 consecutive deliveries in Abidjan. Anthropometric data of newborns, mothers and placentas. *Helvetica Paediatrica Acta (Supplementum).*

Reinhardt, M. C., P. Ambroise-Thomas, R. Cavallo-Serra, C. Meylan, and R. Gautier (in press). Malaria at delivery in Abidjan. *Helevetica Peadiatrica Acta (Supplementum).*

Richards, A. (1932) *Hunger and work in a savage tribe.* Routledge, London.

Roll, S. (1970) Conservation of Number: A comparison between cultures and subcultures, *Revta, interam, psicol.,* 4(1), pp. 13–18.

Segall, M. H., D. T. Campbell, and M. J. Herskovits (1966) *The influence of culture on visual perception.* Bobbs-Merril Co., Indianapolis.

Serpell, R. (1969a) Cultural differences in attentional preference for colour over form, *Int. J. Psychol.,* 4, pp. 1–8.

Serpell, R. (1969b) The Influence of Language, Education and Culture on Attentional Preference between Colour and Form, *Int. J. Psychol.,* 4, pp. 183–194.

Serpell, R. (1976) *Culture's influence on behaviour.* Methuen, London.

Shayer, M. (1972) Conceptual Demands in the Nuffield O-Level Physics Course, *Sch. Sci. Rev.* 54, pp. 26–34.

Sieye, A. (1975) *Le développement psychobiologique de l'enfant ouest-africain. Malnutrition, environnement, stimulation et développement chez l'enfant de 0 à 4 ans dans la région d'Abidjan en 1970–1974.* Thèse inédite, 2 Vol., Univ. René Descartes, Paris.

Stock, M. B., and P. M. Smythe (1967) The effect of undernutrition during infancy on subsequent brain growth and intellectual development. *Sth. Afr. Med. J.,* 41, pp. 1027–30.

Stone, L. J., H. T. Smith, and L. B. Murphy (Eds.) (1974) *The competent infant*, Tavi-stock, London.

Super, C. M. (1976) Environmental effects on motor development: the case of "African infant precocity" *Developmental Medicine and Child Neurology*, 18, 5, pp. 561–567.

Super, C. M. (in prep.) Behavioural development in infancy. In R. L. Munroe, R. H. Munroe and B. B. Whiting (Eds.), *Handbook of cross-cultural human development*. Garland Press, New York.

Szeminska, A. (1965) The Evolution of Thought: Some Applications of Research Findings to Educational Practice, *Monogr. Soc. Res. Child. Dev.*, 30(2), pp. 47–57.

Taiwo, C. O. (1968) Primary School Mathematics in African Societies. Commonwealth Conference on Mathematics in Schools. Commonwealth Secretariat, London.

Tapé, G. (1977) Les activités de classification et les opérations logiques chez les enfants ivoiriens. *Ann. Univ. Abidjan, Serie* D., 10, pp. 155–163.

UNECSO (1976) *Final Report: Conference of Ministers of Education of African Member States*. Lagos (Nigeria), January 27–February 4, 1976.

UNICEF (1967) *Strategy for children. A study of UNICEF assistance policies*. UNICEF, New York.

UNICEF (1972) Enfance, jeunesse, femmes et plans de developpement: la conférence de Lomé. *Carnets de l'enfance/Assignment children*, 20.

UNICEF (1977) *Annual Report*. UNICEF, New York.

Uzgiris, I. C. (1964) Situational Generality of Conservation, *Child Dev.* 35, pp. 831–841.

Uzgiris, I. C. (1976) Organization of sensorimotor intelligence. In M. Lewis (Ed.), *Origins of Intelligence*. Plenum Press, New York. pp. 123–164.

Uzgiris, I. C. and J. McV. Hunt (1975) *Assessment in infancy: ordinal scales of psycho-logical development*. Univ. of Illinois Press, Urbana.

Valantin, S. (1970) Le développement de la fonction manipulatoire chez l'enfant sénéga-lais au cours des deux premières années de la vie. Thèse de 3ème cycle, Univ. de Paris.

Valantin, S. (1972) Problems raised by observations of children in various cultural environments. *Early Child Development and Care*, 2, 3, pp. 276–89.

Vernon, P. E. (1965) Environmental Handicaps and Intellectual Development. *Br. J. Educ. Psychol.*, 35, 9–20m, pp. 117–126.

Vernon, P. E. (1969) *Intelligence and Cultural Environment*. Methuen, London.

Vouilloux, D. (1959) Etude de la psychomotricité d'enfants Africains au Cameroun: Test de Gesell et réflexes archaïques. *J. De la Soc. des Africanistes*, 29, pp. 11–18.

Warren, N. (1972) African infant precocity. *Psychol. Bull.* 78, 5, pp. 353–367.

Warren, N. and J. M. Parkin (1974) A neurological and behavioural comparison of African and European newborns in Uganda. *Child Development*, 45, pp. 966–971.

Waterlow, J. C. (1972) Classification and definition of protein-calorie malnutrition. *Brit. Medical J.*, 3, pp. 5826, 566–569.

Wellcome, Working Party (1970) Classification of infantile malnutrition. *Lancet*, 2, p. 302.

Werner, E. (1972) Infants around the world: Cross-cultural studies of psychomotor development from birth to two years. *J. Cross-cult. Psych.* 3, 2, pp. 111–134.

Whiting, B. (1976) The problem of the packaged variable. In K. F. Reigel and J. A. Meacham (Eds.), *The developing individual in a changing world* Vol. I. Mouton, The Hague. pp. 303–309.

Winick, (1969) Malnutrition and brain development. *J. Ped.*, 74, 5, pp. 667–679.

Witkin, H. A., and J. W. Berry (1975) Psychological-differentiation in cross-cultural perspective. *J. of Cross-cultural Psychol.*, 6, pp. 4–87.

Witkin, H. A., R. B. Dyk, H. F. Faterson, D. R. Goodenough, and S. A. Karp (1962) *Psychological differentiation: studies of development.* Wiley, New York. New Edition: L. Erlbaum, Potomac, Md. 1974.

Wober, M. (1975) *Psychology in Africa.* International African Institute, London.

Zagré, A. (1976) *Approche de l'enfant en milieu traditionnel voltaique.* Université de Ouagadougou, mimeo.

Zempléni, A., and J. Zempléni-Rabain (1972) In F. Duyckaerts, C. B. Hindley, I. Lézine, M. Reuchlin, and A. Zempléni *Milieu et développement.* P. U. F., Paris. pp. 151–213.

Zempléni-Rabain, J. (1966) Modes fondamentaux de relation chez l'enfant Wolof, du sevrage à l'integration dans la classe d'age. *Psychopathologie Africaine,* 2, 2, pp. 143–177.

Zempléni-Rabain, J. (1968) L'aliment et la stratégie de l'apprentissage de l'échange avec les frères chez l'enfant Wolof. *Psychopathologie Africaine,* 4, 2, pp. 297–311.

Zempléni-Rabain, J. (1970) L'enfant Wolof de 2 à 5 ans (Sénégal). Echanges corporels et échanges médiatisés par les objects. *Revue de Neuro-psychiatrie infantile,* 18, 10–11, pp. 785–798.

Zempléni-Rabain, J. (1973) Food and the strategy involved in learning fraternal exchange among Wolof children. In P. Alexandre (Ed.), *French perspectives in African studies.* Oxford Univ. Press, London. pp. 221–234.

REFERENCES